P9-DWQ-284

Praise for *Becoming Aware*

*"I've always known Lisa Garr was a special person,
but I had no idea—until reading her book—of all the things
she'd lived through to become the bright light she is today.
There is something very wise and embracing about Lisa—
when she showers you with that profound kindness of hers,
it changes you. Now everybody who reads Becoming Aware
can have that experience, and we'll all be better off for it. I've
been hoping Lisa would take her great talents and express
them in the words of a book, and I'm delighted to help tell
all the world that it's here. This book is like taking a marvel-
ous journey with a wonderful new friend, and what she
reveals on your adventure will stay with you forever."*

— **Marianne Williamson**, author of *A Return to Love*

*"Becoming Aware will give you the tools for and inspire
you to visualize your ideal future. Lisa will take you from
where you are to where you need to be. I strongly encourage
you to get a copy of this book."*

— **Jack Canfield**, originator of the
Chicken Soup for the Soul® series

*"I've known Lisa for many, many years and everything she
does is in the light. Becoming Aware is her story and much
more. She shares how a tragedy helped her to open her heart
and her clairvoyance, and to become aware."*

— **Doreen Virtue**, founder of Angel Therapy®
and author of over 50 books

Becoming
Aware

Hay House Titles of Related Interest

Becoming Aware

How to Repattern Your Brain
and Revitalize Your Life

LISA GARR

HAY HOUSE, INC.
Carlsbad, California • New York City
London • Sydney • Johannesburg
Vancouver • Hong Kong • New Delhi

Published and distributed in the United States by: Hay House, Inc.: www.hayhouse.com® • *Published and distributed in Australia by:* Hay House Australia Pty. Ltd.: www.hayhouse.com.au • *Published and distributed in the United Kingdom by:* Hay House UK, Ltd.: www.hay house.co.uk • *Published and distributed in the Republic of South Africa by:* Hay House SA (Pty), Ltd.: www.hayhouse.co.za • *Distributed in Canada by:* Raincoast Books: www.raincoast.com • *Published in India by:* Hay House Publishers India: www.hayhouse.co.in

Cover design: Nita Ybarra • *Interior design:* Riann Bender
Interior photos: Courtesy of the author

The stories in this book are true; however, some names and identifying details have been changed to preserve confidentiality.

The author of this book does not dispense medical advice or prescribe the use of any technique as a form of treatment for physical, emotional, or medical problems without the advice of a physician, either directly or indirectly. The intent of the author is only to offer information of a general nature to help you in your quest for emotional and spiritual well-being. In the event you use any of the information in this book for yourself, the author and the publisher assume no responsibility for your actions.

Library of Congress Cataloging-in-Publication Data

Garr, Lisa.
  Becoming aware : how to repattern your brain and revitalize your life / Lisa Garr.
    pages cm
  ISBN 978-1-4019-4726-2 (hardback)
  1. Change (Psychology) 2. Self-realization. 3. Awareness. 4. Conduct of life. 5. Spiritual life. I. Title.
  BF637.C4G375 2015
  158--dc23
                        2014043476

Hardcover ISBN: 978-1-4019-4726-2

10 9 8 7 6 5 4 3 2 1
1st edition, May 2015

Printed in the United States of America

<u>Becoming Aware</u> is dedicated to my husband, Jon Davis, and our amazing daughter, Kayla Davis; and to my loving parents, Edward and Danielle Garr.

Contents

Foreword

I am truly overjoyed to comment briefly on Lisa Garr's magnificent book, which you now hold in your hands. It has been several decades now that I have known and admired this remarkable woman. During these years I have persistently encouraged Lisa to go public with her exceptional personal story, and by doing so offer a bright ray of hope for many people who have lived through traumatizing events similar to her own. After a near-death accident while engaged in competitive mountain-bike racing, Lisa undertook the seemingly insurmountable task of retraining her brain so that she could regain all of her physical and mental capacities. She successfully undertook this mission with the same ardor and enthusiasm that is evident on every page of this remarkable book.

I first met Lisa as a guest on her groundbreaking radio show in Los Angeles called *The Aware Show.* The story of this show personifies the story of Lisa's life.

As a young doctoral student, I was blessed to come into contact with the teachings of the late Dr. Abraham Maslow, who dedicated his life to the nurturing of an approach to living called self-actualization. I was enthralled by his radical idea that there are people among us who reach exalted states of awareness and live exciting lives impacting the world they live in and the people around them. I made it my life's purpose to not only learn as much as I could about Maslow's ideas, but to incorporate them into my own life as well. Maslow described and taught about the inner calling of these kinds of people to become everything that they are capable of becoming, and how difficult to impossible it is for them to stifle this drive. They become restless and discontented unless they are doing what they are "fitted for." The need for self-actualization, Maslow says, can be summed up as: "What a man *can* be, he *must* be."

One of the most prominent features of self-actualizers is what Maslow called a "detachment from outcome." That is, these are people who are not motivated by external enticements. These are "growth motivated" people, who listen to their inner desires rather than any reward that might accrue to them as a result of following what their inner voices dictate. They do not live or work for external rewards such as fame, financial remuneration, status, or merit badges of any sort. They follow their heart . . . and this is the story of the Lisa Garr I have come to know, admire, and love.

More than 15 years ago Lisa felt compelled to start a radio show interviewing the most influential movers and shakers in the field of human development and higher consciousness. This show ultimately became the must-stop for any and all authors on book tours, including yours truly on many, many occasions over the years. There was no budget for this show, so Lisa did all of the work necessary to bring this show to the public at her own expense. She was not motivated by any external outcome, only an insatiable inner passion to learn from those who were excelling at the top of their field and making a difference in the world. Imagine that—working every day for 15-plus years, recording all of her interviews, and doing it because she was listening to the voice of her own life's dharma.

I have sat with many of the world's most accomplished interviewers, and I consider Lisa to be my all-time favorite. Over a period of 40 years I have also endured many an interview that I was not thrilled about doing. But whenever I see on my itinerary that I'll be live on *The Aware Show* with Lisa Garr, I know that it will be a stimulating hour for myself and, most important, the audience as well. She always brings a kind of loving energy and excitement to every subject matter. Rather than asking a series of prepared questions, she does her homework thoroughly and then engages in a stimulating conversation that is over all too soon. You will find this same compelling energy on every page of this provocative book as well.

I am so proud of Lisa for completing the monumental task of writing this book. It is filled with what she calls "Awarisms," which are quick tips for increasing one's level of awareness on the spot. The story of her near-death experience and her subsequent voyage of recovery in retraining her brain is an unforgettable bonus.

I know this woman as a peerless professional, a dedicated mother, and a personal friend. Simply put, she is the best of the best. She embodies what my spiritual mentor Henry David Thoreau meant when he urged us from his cabin in the woods at Walden Pond—where he lived for two years, two months, and two days, on land owned by his friend and mentor Ralph Waldo Emerson—that "if one advances confidently in the direction of his dreams, and endeavors to live the life which he has imagined, he will meet with a success unexpected in common hours."

I am so pleased that Lisa chose to advance confidently in the direction of her own dreams. The treasure you are about to read will be life enhancing, I guarantee it. And this too I hypothesize: had Ralph Waldo Emerson and Henry David Thoreau taken their classic works on a book tour back in the 19th century, and had there been an *Aware Show* with Lisa Garr to visit, they assuredly would have made it their business to be there.

I enthusiastically endorse this great work and am proud to lend my name in helping as many people as possible to receive the benefits of what is written here.

Love,
I AM, Wayne Dyer

✳ ✴ ✳

Preface

This is what I remember after the accident that tried to make me forget:

I'm flat on my back, but I'm not staring up at blue mountain sky. My vantage point is turned around and I'm looking down at my passed-out body on the ground beneath me. The emergency medical technicians say that I am hurt. I am perhaps even dead, but the feeling sweeping over my soul isn't one of fear or sorrow.

It's pure euphoria.

My damaged body is a mere distraction as I feel and hear the thoughts and urgent words of the EMTs assisting what remains of me. In fact, I'm quite in tune with these women and men—I can feel which one is off purpose, which one is yearning for love, and what their unfulfilled desires are in life. The experience I'm having is that of pure expanded consciousness, where there are no boundaries of skin or the body, or even of a location.

Everything up here is one. I can sense and feel Asia randomly, as if it suddenly came to me instead of my flying across the world to another continent. Anything that is in my awareness is instantly manifested in my awareness.

*I know I've had some sort of terrible accident be-
cause my body is unconscious and throwing up at the
same time, being held sideways by the magnificent
first responders so that I don't choke. They listen to my
heart. Look concerned. Try to find a pulse. I can't feel
any of this because I'm in the most peaceful place of
expanded consciousness I have ever known. This image
is etched in my mind in a crystal clear way.*

*Somehow I know that if I don't get back into my
body soon, this place will become too comfortable, too
easy. Yet I don't want to leave.*

*I continue to watch as a man runs up next to my
body and one of the EMTs says, "Are you Jon? She's
been asking for you." Before I can process those partic-
ulars, I see a silver type of cord filled with light attach
from my body to his, connecting the two of us. At that
moment, I realize that I need to let him know I'm okay.*

*Slowly, I open my eyes, and from my perspective on
the ground below, everything is blurry. I see Jon, the ex-
boyfriend I went to the race with that day. I can't talk
or acknowledge him because words refuse to come out.
All I want to do is get my message across and then go
back to that peaceful place where there was no pain, no
struggle, no frustration, only neutrality. I communicate
this to Jon with my eyes; it's a different type of communication that needs no words, and is far more effective.
I know in my deepest heart that he understands I must
leave. I must.*

*I close my eyes and exit again, only to return to my
place above as the end of my life continues to unfold.*

There is a moment during any mountain-bike race where the connection between the rider and bike becomes almost spiritual. The minute your feet clip into the pedals and the wind hits your face, you are in another world. The tires spin, rubber grips dirt, and you're off!

I was a competitive mountain biker for many years and have a routine that suits me: I don't listen to music or words. Instead, I do something that many might find odd in our technology-loving society. I turn off, turn inward, and listen only to my own thoughts. Buffeted by complete silence, I always hear the tires grinding, the wind whispering, and a little voice inside of my head urging, "Up, up, up." As I climb toward the top of the mountain, it's never about getting to the destination, but that journey up.

I love that during this part of the trip, I can let my mind go. During those heady moments, my deepest, innermost thoughts come rushing to the surface, as if they've been uncaged. It's like they've always been waiting there for the right moment, and a slow, steady climb up rough terrain is the optimal time to throw open those mental gates. With the sun warming my face, it's safe to connect with nature, God, and anything else that will let me expand and fully be myself.

I've often thought that mountain biking is an analogy for life. You decide to take this ride, but first gaze up at a daunting-looking incline. Frankly, it seems impossible to climb, but for some reason you're "in" before you know you're in. That's the birth and childhood stage. Getting to the top is like the grind of the following years—you have to make it past all of the obstacles along the way to get to your personal mountaintop.

And there it is. Just a few more pushes of the pedal, and suddenly the mountaintop is within your grasp. When the ground levels and you can't climb any higher, it's just you, the blue sky, and a feeling of immense victory. That feeling is so powerful that it's like a jolt from God.

For most of us, however, life isn't an easy, straight ascent. There are roots, rocks, ruts, and cliffs on our climb. They are placed there to wake us up, teach us, or maybe trip us up, thus throwing us off course in a major way. Make it past them, and getting to the top is an even sweeter victory. Of course, once we do get to the top, some bikers joke that "it's all downhill from here."

I know about a downward slide. My name is Lisa Garr, and I literally fell down a mountain and nearly lost my life. It was one of the best things to ever happen to me. But we'll get to that part in a minute.

First things first: As a competitive mountain biker, I had been racing for the California state championship, and due to the 104-degree heat and a long, very challenging course, my body became severely dehydrated. Imagine reaching the top of a mountain, knowing that you're about two miles from the finish and about to take over the lead, and then blacking out while you're pedaling at top speeds.

I don't remember my body tumbling off the bike and hitting the rocky ground below. Doctors would later tell me that my head smashed against that unforgiving terrain so hard and so often that it bounced up and down like a ball, injuring my brain in the process.

Ask me the rest of what I can recall about that day and the answers aren't that easy. Frankly, I don't remember a big portion of it, which is a completely normal response considering that memory loss is retroactive in most traumatic events.

It's really frightening when you reach for a thought and it isn't there. Or someone reminds you of a conversation you just conducted and you can't remember you even spoke to that person. I started to lose trust in my own brain. And it was embarrassing when people would have to remind me of what I said or did or promised to do tomorrow. When you hurt your brain, the answers aren't always so easy.

Yet I was ultimately able to repattern my brain and revitalize my life. I wrote this book to share my healing process, as well as what I learned throughout. I hope you'll draw inspiration from my story to overcome any challenges you might be facing. I am living proof that life is full of amazing possibilities.

* * *

Introduction

Today, the person I am is so different from the one I was before my biking accident. I now host and produce a popular syndicated radio show called *The Aware Show*, heard in the Los Angeles market on KPFK 90.7 FM or on KPFK.org. Or you might know me from a series I host for Gaiam TV called *Gaiam Inspirations*. I have a show on Hay House Radio called *Being Aware*, as well as one of the largest telesummit series on the Internet. And I am a weekend host on *Coast to Coast AM*, syndicated in over 500 stations around the world. Combined, I reach millions of listeners globally a month.

On *The Aware Show*, I interview influential and incredible new-thought leaders from a variety of scientific and spiritual pursuits. In the upcoming chapters of this book, I want to help you transform your life by teaching you how I applied 15 years of these experts' lessons to my own life as a businesswoman, wife, and mother.

Helping others and myself become more aware is undeniably my purpose, as is letting people know that they have choices when it comes to their healing. Most important, I want them to know that they don't have to live their lives with emotional pain. I can't do anything else, especially after experiencing the most pure sense of consciousness and expansion I have ever known.

Here is my story in a nutshell. (I will expand on it more in later chapters, but I want to set this journey in motion.) A constant athlete and dancer from childhood, in college I taught aerobics and then spinning classes. But that wasn't enough. To challenge myself, I took up mountain biking and then connected with a group of friends in the entertainment business who introduced me to competitive racing. Instantly, I was hooked.

Exercise has always been a way to elevate my mood and connect with my goals—and I knew that there was a lot more I wanted to achieve in that area. In the meantime, I started taking classes in intuition and meditation, developing my intuitive abilities over time. One of the first lessons I learned was that you cannot help other people see their issues unless you see and heal those matching issues in yourself.

One day after a race, I met a man named Jon and we began dating, sharing our passion for mountain-bike racing. A few years later, after a rocky relationship as a result of my acting out my unresolved issues from childhood, we broke up. Nevertheless, we agreed to go to the final race of the state championship series together to support each other. I was in second place in the entire state of California when I passed out during the final lap of the race and fell down a long, steep hill.

I was unconscious for about 30 minutes, and it was the most peaceful and transformational experience of my life. It was in this place that I learned about how our consciousness is truly connected.

In the end, I decided to stay and fight for my life. My body was airlifted out of the ravine and taken to the closest hospital. I was so dehydrated that eight bags of saline were pumped into my body before I regained full consciousness.

I may have been conscious, but I had damaged the part of my brain responsible for language and couldn't say a thing. A cold feeling of helpless panic kicked in because I wanted to talk, but the words would not come out. Jon, who had rushed to the hospital after me, became my voice.

I tried to put back together my brain and my life. After several months of recovering on my own, I started working with a very cutting-edge type of electroencephalogram (EEG) technology that sent a signal to the damaged areas of my brain, asking it to respond to positive images. Luckily, my thought-wave patterns acted in a productive and encouraging manner, but just not all of the time.

When my brain waves weren't sending the proper frequency because they were dormant (my right prefrontal cortex was still damaged from the injury), the non-signal was recognized and the program would then send back a signal to my brain, teaching it how to wake itself up again. Think of it like doing a push-up—at first you can only do one or two, but you work your way up to many more as you develop the muscles.

This technique was being used on people with ADHD, autism, and brain traumas, and like me, those people were getting well from these exercises. That's when I realized there is scientific evidence that our thoughts create our own reality and that self-healing is possible.

I also learned that it is an ongoing process, and we need to constantly tune up our awareness and stay committed to our own self-healing process through our thoughts and actions.

I CAME BACK FROM MY ACCIDENT realizing how important the brain is in our personal development, especially when you combine cutting-edge, brain-transforming techniques with spiritual lessons. So in the chapters of this book, I will explain how to combine body and spirit in order to live a 100 percent conscious day filled with awareness. My goal is that you no longer walk around in a crisis-filled, *what-do-I-do?*, stressed-out state that invites illness by weakening your immune system. Instead, imagine a life filled with work you enjoy, balanced by relationships that are loving, fulfilling, and solid as you revitalize your life and health in several ways.

Becoming Aware is broken down into two parts, with the first one focusing on how I found my own awareness as a young girl who survived several early challenges. Luckily, these experiences brought me to a place of spirituality combined with a yearning to experience personal growth. I will also go into detail about how I healed both my brain and my body after my traumatic bike accident. Perhaps most important, though, I will explain how I healed my *life* and committed myself to a loving, aware relationship with Jon (who is now my husband) and later with our daughter, Kayla.

In the second part, I will tackle some of the big topics I discuss on the radio and in my work, including becoming aware of your own potential while dealing with the soaring stress levels of modern life. I'm just like you in that not everything runs as I've planned. That's why I wrote a chapter about what to do when life hits you on the head or when you come up against roadblocks. I'll provide tips for how to cope with loss, which is something we tend to rush through in our society instead of truly experience. I believe that a healthy body is the foundation for an aware life, so I'll give you my personal tips on how to create a body and brain that will serve you well into the future. I'll share my views of how to stay aware in love despite a world that pulls us in so many directions. And since having a child completely changed my life, I'll also provide my best conscious-parenting tips.

Both this book and my shows are designed to offer lasting, transformative, and soul-searching change while bringing the latest information to everyone. The shows are my passion, and they have taken on a momentum of their own while helping so many people from around the globe heal and become more aware. Suicides have been prevented, and people have reconnected with family members while also finding work and a lifestyle that gives them great joy. Major healing has occurred for people who listen, both in their physical selves and in their relationships, including romantic love and family interactions.

My work is not work. It's my life's passion. It's why I'm here. My purpose is to communicate messages that inspire positive growth and change.

Of course, sometimes I make it at 100 percent; other days it's only 80 percent. I try to remember that we're all only human! So in the upcoming pages, I'll give you practical, real-world ways to help you live a more conscious life, which doesn't require perfection. Again, it's all about opening your eyes and becoming aware. To that end, I will also be offering you tips I like to call "Awarisms" to give you a quick hit of mindfulness in that moment. Feel free to go back to those Awarisms when you need a reminder to be conscious.

By the way, you don't have to hit your head to start this journey. Just turn the page!

* * *

Part I

My Story of Becoming Aware

CHAPTER I

Remembering the Past

If my last name sounds familiar to you, that's because Garr is a name that has been up in lights and in movie credits for quite some time. I was raised in an entertainment family, with a grandmother who was an original Radio City Music Hall Rockette and an aunt who's a successful actress (and one of my early role models). Most people know Aunt Teri from movies like *Tootsie, Young Frankenstein, Mr. Mom, Close Encounters of the Third Kind,* and *The Black Stallion,* just to name a few of her hits.

My parents were childhood sweethearts who lived the traditional American dream. They met in junior high school and fell deeply in love, and later came marriage and deployment. My dad was an Army physician, which meant that he was immediately sent away to a faraway place called Vietnam. He did several tours tending to the wounded soldiers, saving some and sadly losing others.

We moved around a lot when I was really young, bouncing from Army base to Army base, and it was hard not to feel uprooted. My mother was often forced to act as a single parent while her mate was at war, so his ultimate return was cause for celebration and reevaluation. It wasn't surprising that he came home with his own wounds, but these were the kind that you couldn't see and weren't treated. No one in those days had really heard of a by-product of war called *post-traumatic stress disorder,* and any signs of anxiety or discomfort coming from those who had served were swept under the rug. My mother, my brother, and I had our own diagnosis, though: we knew that the head of our house was somehow "broken" by this horrifying war.

My father worked diligently to put his professional and personal life back together and live the promise of that perfect American dream in the suburbs with his beautiful wife—who was a special-needs teacher and later an entrepreneur with her own design business—and children. We still moved quite a bit after Dad came home; then when I was five, we settled in Cleveland, where he started his own medical practice.

I remember that we had 11 trees in our backyard, and my brother and I used to eat our lunches seated atop one of them, which we affectionately named "Kevin" for some reason that I can't remember. On weekends, we spent our time in the charming village of Chagrin Falls, Ohio. From the look of it, we were the picture-postcard, all-American family. Yet behind closed doors, there was quite a bit of tension in our family as we readjusted after my father's homecoming, as many families did in similar situations.

When I look back on my own imperfect past, I don't do so with blame because there is no point, as it makes no sense whatsoever. No, my dad didn't cope very well with the stresses of being a young man just back from war, who was trying to create a life for himself and his family. He wasn't home a lot in those days, and my mother tried to compensate by being both parents. Having said that, my parents did the best they could under difficult circumstances, much like countless other Vietnam War veterans and their spouses.

My father worked incredibly hard as a physician and was very admired. He was always a great doctor, a true healer, and he never took a day off in his 38-year-long medical career. Meanwhile, my mother did everything possible to make it all work despite the PTSD, which I believe Dad still suffers from. To this day, whenever someone slams a door, he will jump almost out of his skin like he's heard a bomb go off. It seems that he's never been able to rid himself of the sound of those life-stealing explosions in the middle of the night.

What happens when fixing the human body is your job, and sometimes you can't because it's just unfixable? This is why I believe that war victims are not only those who have lost their lives. In many ways, my father lost the early, bright-eyed promise of his own stress-free existence.

When I was eight, we moved to Orange County, California, where Dad started another practice with a group of doctors. In many ways, all of our lives now seemed to be set. My mother appeared to be the perfect housewife, but she was never the type to just sit around. Mom worked really hard, which also instilled in me the idea that hard work was key.

Dad's patients loved him, and he even played comedy tapes in the ER before their operations. When we would visit him at work, the nurses and medical professionals always said that my father was "one of the great doctors." He was a great doctor when it came to his own family, too.

I remember when I was in my early 20s and living alone, I came down with a rapid fever, which was strange because I was usually a healthy athlete. I was lying on the couch when my fever suddenly spiked to 103 degrees and a brutal pain set into my spine.

I called my dad and said, "I'm feeling so awful." He diagnosed me over the phone: "You have spinal meningitis and need to get to the hospital right now." Hearing the anxious tone of my father's voice, I drove myself and found that his diagnosis was right after a spinal tap told us the news. Dad saved my life that day, because without quick medical attention and medication to bring down that fever, I could have easily died.

Unfortunately when I was a child, there were other wounds that didn't heal so well. Most likely as a defense mechanism, my mother approached things from a negative stance. She always anticipated the worst thing happening and then was never disappointed if it did. Mom's negativity became part of my own subconscious programming, and I have worked very hard over the years to stop that sort of thinking from becoming my default mode. I'm aware of it—and aware of how to reverse it. In other words, I have consciously worked at breaking the pattern. I have learned how to break negative patterns and build new neural networks in my brain of the pattern I choose to create. (This is one of the types of things I call "Awarisms," and you'll see many more of them throughout the book.)

On a positive note, my mother also demonstrated adaptability and resilience. She is a very creative and strong woman who taught me independence and fortitude. Today we laugh about my tumultuous past, including being a sensitive child in an environment that was less than perfect. Just like so many families of the post-Vietnam era, we basically shoved a lot of things under the carpet that were later recognized as traumatic. In those years, the men didn't seek counseling, as they were in denial that anything was wrong. They simply had to be men and get on with their lives.

In my parents' defense, and I love them both dearly, they didn't have words or theories about "conscious parenting" back in those days. They weren't given tools to cope with family life or access to an Internet with scads of helpful stories and theories. They just had what they learned from their own parents coupled with the struggles of their modern lives. They provided an incredible life for my brother and me, and are both amazing people and wonderful role models in their own way. They taught me strength, leadership, forgiveness, and how to love. However, I didn't realize all of this until much, much later on.

As far as my brother is concerned, he turned out to be an immensely creative artist and brilliant inventor. We have our parents to thank for our drive to succeed and our love for nature. In those early days, though, it wasn't so easy to recognize these lessons. As I entered my teen years, I didn't know how to look inward, but instead acted out in different ways.

As a young adolescent, my body began to rapidly develop, and I had a C-cup bra size by age 12. In other words, it wasn't exactly hard to get attention, even though I was a bit shy and didn't want *that* kind of attention.

As I grew up and the curves firmly settled into place, I found certain times of my life to be a brutal experience. In middle school, for example, the theme of my life seemed to be: *Don't let your light shine too bright; play small to slip under the radar.* The joy, charisma, and enthusiasm I was born with as a member of an entertainment family didn't fit into the model of Catholic school at the time. I was a good performer thanks to my mother, who drove me to three hours of jazz, tap, and ballet four days a week after school for years.

My principal and a group of the nuns at school decided to take out their ideology on me because they disliked that I was a performer. The message I received was that they didn't like me being talented or shining my own bright light. I was even called into the principal's office once for being "stuck-up and conceited." This was on the tail of winning Miss Cheer USA after my advisor at the school asked me to show a bit of my routine to the student body during an assembly. This was a punishable event.

I don't want to sound like I'm slamming the nuns. I admire and respect those who take the oath of service. I just ran into people who didn't honor my talents or encourage me to explore them.

When I got to high school, I continued as a cheerleader, and I won a national dance competition. None of this really surprised anyone in my family because they knew I was driven and capable, which are two formidable traits that certainly made me stand out from the pack. This is the good stuff I got from my parents, as they always instilled in me a strong work ethic and the importance of setting goals.

So from the outside looking in, my high-school life seemed to be on the right track . . . until, that is, the bottom fell out.

On a warm spring weekend, there was a party down at the beach. It was one of those times as a young girl where your dad drops you off with that warning to "be careful," and the assurance that he would be "back to get you around 10." It's hard to tell this story because it's still so painful and embarrassing, but here goes.

That night, I was standing on the beach in a sea of classmates. Someone must have called the cops because suddenly there was a police helicopter overhead coming to break up the party. In a panic, kids began to scramble and ran under the trees to hide. In a blind rush, I raced under a tree where several guys were already hiding. In the dark, I could feel hands all over my body. They weren't welcome hands, but intruding ones. Gasping and crying, I ran away as quickly as possible before this escalated into an even more horrifying situation.

The next week at school, my entire life changed.

My coach informed me that I was kicked off the cheerleading squad. Apparently a rumor was going around that I slept with seven boys underneath that tree at the party. The administration of this particular Catholic high school irresponsibly took gossip as fact and changed my life in a moment. I was on top of the world as one of the most talented kids in school, and then shoved to the bottom as they branded me as someone of low moral fiber.

Just like so many girls who are victims of sexual assault, or in this case perceived sexual interaction, I hid my face in shame—even though I was attacked and absolutely did not have sex with any of these boys (who went unpunished). In those days, I wasn't good at defending myself, nor could I turn to my parents because I was too mortified. Even my brother couldn't figure out what had happened. At lunch, no one would sit with me. In class, heads turned the other way. I could hear the whispers and my face would flame red. *How could they think this about me?* I'd wonder. *Don't they know the truth?*

There was only one place on campus where I could go during breaks and not find any ridicule: the chapel. I didn't sit on the pews, but rather found solace in the actual confessional area. The priest wasn't there at the time. In fact, nobody knew I was in there.

I wasn't alone, though. I was there with God. And during this time, I developed an amazing relationship with the divine and learned lifelong tools for inner strength.

"Why, God, did this happen to me?" I'd ask.

The answer didn't come in words, but in people who eventually entered the chapel. They were members of a religious group that liked to hang out where *I* liked to hang out during school breaks. I got to know these kids and tagged along with them, affectionately calling them "the God Squad."

It didn't take long before my new friends asked me what had happened that night on the beach. I explained to them that the guys were a bit drunk and very grabby. "Really, I'm going to have sex with seven boys while hiding from a helicopter at a huge party?" I said. "I knew I was in a bad place and ran away." The God Squad didn't judge. They didn't look at me as someone with a tarnished reputation, but as the victim of gossip.

Being a scorned teenager, I lost my normal high-school life in my senior year. Yet what I found was far more profound because I tapped into my own spirituality. My inner strength grew, and I deepened my relationship with Spirit. Something else happened internally during this time, too, which was learning that shame, guilt, and fear were the cause of many people's most unresolved issues. I was experiencing them for myself, and when I reached out to my new friends, I was amazed to learn that these three emotions were so universally felt.

Despite my friendship with the God Squad, I couldn't wait for high school to end. I'll never forget leaving the graduation ceremony with my cap and gown on, speeding down the freeway with pure joy in my heart. I had a dance performance to get to, so I was in a hurry as well. A cop pulled me over, but my joy was so contagious that he couldn't even write me a ticket. Instead, he said, "Miss, I'll escort you to your performance. Congratulations on graduating."

It was one of my best presents, plus a moment in life when I truly felt supported by the universe. And even better, I felt free.

As I look back on my teenage years, I know now that human beings develop our framework for how we see ourselves—perhaps in a forever way—during that turbulent time. Even without an experience as dramatic as my night on the beach, I still might have branded myself in ways that could have stuck for life. We form those lasting decisions in our youth, and in many ways we're like cows taking a branding iron to ourselves. Imagine if I would have believed in gossip and branded myself as a slut or someone who was stupid. I felt fear from my situation and loneliness, but I refused to take on those other labels. This is a good example of an Awarism: in this case, I took an experience from my past where I made a decision about myself that was incorrect or imposed on me and reframed it as a learning experience or a turning point for something good to happen in my life.

I know that my pain in my younger years was the universe's way of saying, "Your path in life is not to be a cheerleader. We will give you a dramatic U-turn that will shout to your former life, 'I'm out of here!'" My life's path was to become a spiritual teacher, but not through the typical ways. What I couldn't know then was that my ways of doing it would be through media, where I would illuminate different teachings and paths.

MY NEXT STOP AFTER HIGH SCHOOL was the University of Southern California. My minor was dance because performing still lurked in the back of my mind, but I also wanted to write and communicate with people on a large scale. I decided to major in broadcast journalism, and USC's Annenberg School of Communication was one of the best places for this in the country. I also knew that I wanted to spend the rest of my life in charge of my own destiny because my life was so out of control when I was in high school.

While in college, I auditioned for acting jobs and quickly got work, including recurring roles on TV shows like *Growing Pains*. Soon, my course load became too overwhelming and I thought I'd get more experience actually working than staying in school. I left school with only eight units needed to finish (I will finish my degree someday!).

It wasn't long before I found that acting wasn't my calling. My fate was commonly in the hands of a director or producer or a role in a script I needed to fit—I found there were too many variables that went into whether I got the part or not. One day, I got a call from my agent to go on an audition and it was the first time I said no to him, thus marking the end of my acting career.

Eventually, I changed from someone who wanted to be a dancer and actress to working behind the scenes. By the time I was 23 years old, I was producing segments for *Mike and Maty*, a daytime talk show that was on ABC. These segments were called "Help Me": people would write in for what they needed assistance with, with some of the top requests being a new washing machine or a coveted trip to Disneyland. I really wanted to help these folks, who were often too poor to put food on the table but had big dreams of taking their small children to meet Mickey Mouse.

It seemed to me that the smallest things would bring people the most joy, but what was missing was the joy *inside*. I began to feel like something was missing within me, too.

I decided to start my own business casting audiences, and I still own that company today. You see, what many people don't realize is that TV shows hire companies like mine to fill some of the seats in live studio audiences—and all those chairs need to be filled for every single taping. Production companies can't count on the public just showing up for as many shows as they tape per week, so companies like mine actually have lists of people who are called. The studios need folks to arrive in an organized way and need someone to control that side of production.

Soon I had several clients and hundreds of thousands of dollars flowing through my own company. My business flourished because I was never afraid of hard work, and have always been someone who knows how to form strong teams and empower them (more on that in a later chapter). I was still in show business, but in a way that appealed to me. The work required being on a roller coaster, which was a feeling I knew only too well from my past. In the end, I became someone who could cope, adapt, and survive. In the entertainment business, your life is about all of the above, plus evolving with the times.

No one knew this better than my aunt Teri Garr, and I was privileged to spend time with her when I was growing up. I always wanted to follow in my aunt's footsteps because I was sure she had the greatest life ever. In fact, I'd escape my own life in Orange County and go visit her in nearby Los Angeles, where she would take me out in her red Mercedes 450 SL convertible. We'd go for a facial or a mani-pedi, and everyone would smile as they recognized her. People flocked to her because she was (and still is) so funny. I remember when I was in high school house-sitting for her and driving around town in that cool Mercedes. She found out and got mad, but not *that* mad. I have to admit that she even made me laugh when she was mad at me. Aunt Teri summed it up in a word: *teenagers!*

As a young woman, I could observe my mom and dad through a new lens as well. Although my parents didn't have a lot of consciousness teaching in their early days, I always admired the fact that Dad had us listen to Tony Robbins tapes in the car. That was also my very early introduction to spiritual growth. I was encouraged by Tony's lectures about visualizing what you wanted and then making it happen. I bought a book called *Creative Visualization* by Shakti Gawain, which was all about creating your own reality. This was the first self-help book I read that turned the lightbulb on in my mind. I was like a kid in a candy store when I learned that I could actually create my own reality.

FINDING MY SPIRITUAL SIDE WASN'T EASY in L.A., which I observed in my early days to be a town that exclusively focused on fame and competition. I looked for something deeper because despite the fact that my business filled several needs, my personal life was lacking. The dating scene was a mess, so I decided to spend my free time pursuing something truly worthwhile, which was a meditation class.

A friend of a friend turned me on to the Southern California Psychic Institute, a place that focused on developing your spiritual side. I attended many classes there, where I learned all about meditation and fine-tuning my intuition, as well as how to do psychic readings on other people.

As students, we would sit across from someone else who was having an issue, with the goal of reading their energy. I started to amaze myself because I was able to "see" pictures floating in other people's energy field concerning their past. I got really skilled at it, to the point where even I was shocked. I'd see someone's karma and then communicate what I'd seen so that they could become more aware of why they had created the issue. It was a great challenge and joy to develop my abilities, which also proved very healing when it came to my own psyche.

As an aside, I get to exercise and sharpen those skills on a daily basis now thanks to my radio show. I am constantly using my intuition when I interview guests, and quite often I will intuit what the audience wants to know—listeners regularly tell me that I asked the exact question they were thinking.

Two of my great mentors and friends who were teaching classes back then, Michael and Raphaelle Tamura, have continued to provide me with guidance. They have been with me through every beginning in life: when I started my first radio show, gave birth to my daughter, started my TV show, and moved. Michael is so far ahead of his time in terms of his profound abilities as a spiritual teacher and healer, and so is his wife, Raphaelle. I still consult with them to this day and continue my spiritual journey with both of them as my guides.

In my mid-20s, I was single, running a successful business, becoming a little clearer on what I wanted in life when it came to my business, and knew that the sky was the limit. I was becoming a very conscious entertainment executive. Was that even allowed?

My goal was to have a successful business that was both challenging and paid the bills for my employees and me. To that end, it was a lot of late nights, constant phone calls, and troubleshooting problems to make sure that the business consistently ran smoothly. Yet I'd always wander to the self-help section in the bookstore to figure out what was wrong with me. I had issues with boundaries and found myself in tears a lot of the time. I realize now that it was a lack of consciousness that was holding me back in life.

It would take a hard bump on the head to wake me up.

* ✳ *

CHAPTER 2

My Consciousness Wake-up Call

My aunt Teri was a very good influence in terms of demonstrating how to make your dreams come true in the City of Angels. She may have been one of the biggest stars of her day, so pretty and devastatingly funny, but she was also a smart woman with a great ability to pick the perfect script—like playing Inga in *Young Frankenstein,* Sandy in *Tootsie,* Bobbie in *Oh, God!,* or nervous mom Ronnie in *Close Encounters of the Third Kind.* When I was with her, it was always exciting because her creative friends like Gilda Radner and Carrie Fisher and the great Francis Ford Coppola would come around.

Aunt Teri was never about the fame and fortune, though; she was more about being in full, creative flow, and doing what you were meant to do in this lifetime. She was a gifted comedian and actress, and I loved seeing the creativity that surrounded her while she lived her dreams of performing and writing. She was also a great example to me of what it meant to live your life's work. In other words, she made her *life* her life's work, and her creativity flowed to all aspects of her world, including the amazing design of her house.

When I was breaking into the business, she helped me get a few meetings with agents, and I visited her in New York City, where she was filming a show. During her off-hours, we'd go to comedy clubs and laugh while aspiring talent like Jon Lovitz took the stage, who'd later stop to talk to us because he was her friend. It was a fun and inspirational time, and also a health-focused one. Aunt Teri would take me with her to the Jane Fonda aerobics classes, where the teacher was . . . Jane Fonda! In those days, she had a studio on Robertson Boulevard in Beverly Hills, and the sweat came from some very famous faces.

I was "living the life," as they say in Los Angeles. Yet even when I was running my own business and working on TV shows, I felt a lack of joy and a sense that I wasn't fulfilling my purpose. My favorite place to focus on all of this was in my little beach house, with the sun pouring through the country-cottage windowpanes, where I would reflect on what I truly wanted in life while meditating. I didn't really know what I was doing in those days, but now it's clear to me that I was creating a visualization of *exactly* what I wanted. The business part of my life had promise, but on the personal front, I had several lackluster dates that seemed to lead nowhere special. Just like any other single woman, I wondered if I would ever meet my soul mate or my life would be all about work.

With a lot of energy to put somewhere, I decided to spend my free hours improving my body. To that end, I taught spinning and got into mountain biking with a friend who was an assistant director on one of the shows I had worked on. I found with this sport that you start out with energy to spare and then wind up completely spent by the end of the ride. I joined a group of longtime cyclists, and they had absolutely no mercy on the newbie! Did I mention that these people were pro athletes, which was perfect for me because it pushed me to go harder and improve fast?

I fell in love with it and was soon racing through mountain passes in the middle of nowhere, which felt like heaven after surviving the daily grind of life in crowded L.A. It wasn't long before *I* was the one standing next to the athletes on the podium and accepting my medals, which came as a result of my passion for the sport of mountain biking.

One day, a man about my age approached me and asked, "Don't you have an audience company?"

I nodded.

"I'm Jon, an accountant at one of the production companies. In fact, I cut your checks," he said with a friendly smile.

From the look in his eyes, which were warm and intelligent, I knew that he was someone I needed to get to know. We hung out the rest of the day, and went on to talk for countless hours on the phone. It turned out that he was as passionate about mountain biking as I was, as well as a sixth-degree black belt in Kung Fu San Soo. I did my full questionnaire with this man, including asking him the "big one": *What do you want in life?*

Jon and I went on to date seriously, but although I liked him a lot, I really couldn't focus on him during what I'll call "a rocky time when I wasn't treating men well." It wasn't that I dated other people or purposely hurt his feelings; I just wasn't present in the way that truly mattered. My life revolved around my business and creating my own future, so I wasn't emotionally available. I was in a phase of my life where I was very goal oriented, and my strong will took over when I should have taken a step back and observed the situation. Soon, I would find that it would be impossible to have a loving, lasting, personal life if I didn't get my priorities straight—including making sure that my significant other did, indeed, feel significant.

I'm the first one to admit that I was not treating this man like he deserved to be treated. I'm sure that it was disappointing for him to find that the woman he was falling in love with was completely career driven and had a lack of boundaries in her life when it came to work. So after a few years of this situation, we decided to call it quits and do the proverbial "friend" relationship that follows certain splits.

In fact, Jon agreed to still go with me and offer his support, as I would have for him, at the last race of the seven-series 1999 California State Mountain Bike Championship. It was in my grasp to capture the championship title that September.

THE SETTING OF THE CHAMPIONSHIP RACE was certainly picturesque: Castaic Lake, a reservoir formed by the Castaic Dam in the Sierra Pelona Mountains of northwestern Los Angeles. Action scenes for movies and TV are often filmed there because of the gorgeous but rugged natural terrain, and this is where I arrived for the state championship. I was in second place overall, but this was the last race and counted for double points. I was focused in on my goal of taking the title. It didn't matter to me that when the race started at eight in the morning, it was already a searing 95 degrees. Or that this particular year, they ran the course in a different direction than they had run it in previous years, which would entail far more climbing for the racers.

About 5,300 feet of steep uphill biking was in my future during the 21-mile course.

Hours later, the win was in my reach. The race was three laps, and in the previous two, I'd always passed the first-place girl on the descent. Jon had taught me how to descend, and I was fearless about it. On the third lap, I spotted her right before the descent began, and I knew I'd pass her on the downhill and get to the finish line first.

That was the last thing I remember.

All of a sudden, I woke up at the bottom of the hill with pine needles stuffed into my jersey. My helmet was sideways on my head and cracked in several places (although I didn't know that at the time). I wanted to climb back up the hill, but the pine needles were so thick that I kept slipping.

Another cyclist saw me struggling to get up the hill, stopped, and asked if I was okay. Later, he told me that I was trying to get back on my bike and just kept falling back down the hill. All I remember was pedaling and watching that girl in front of me.

Eventually, doctors would tell me that memory loss is retroactive, and this is why I don't remember the actual fall or trying to scramble back up the hill. I assume that I passed out when I was pedaling due to dehydration—I thought I'd been drinking plenty of water, but it must not have been enough for the heat. I blacked out and fell down a mountain.

What happened next was the most important thing to ever happen to me.

Somehow my body finally dropped to the ground, and I started to float above the entire scene. I was hovering over my body, which was down below me. I could see people surrounding me, but I couldn't really tell what they were doing. Instead, I could tell what they were *feeling*. Some of them were feeling like they were on-purpose in their lives and put here to be emergency medical technicians. Others were off-purpose and wanted to do something else—one wanted to be a painter. I knew that one of the female medics had romantic feelings for one of the male EMTs, but she was too afraid to tell him. I could feel their thoughts, their desires, their unmet needs, but I couldn't hear their voices, as there was no need to do so.

The place I was in was magical. It was vast and pure, with a type of expanded consciousness that I had never experienced before in my life. It was beyond words. I don't even know if there *are* words that could explain the level of consciousness I experienced, something that is much more expansive than anything I've ever known here. I once looked out over the cliff at the great Grand Canyon, and this feeling was even vaster than that experience. When I ask myself why now, I know the answer. This was a place of complete, unconditional love.

There are no conditions of any kind in this state of pure expansion. There are no boundaries; no pain; and no past, present, or future. It is all of those things at once: the past, present, and the future occurring at the same exact time. It is actually a state of all-encompassing awareness rather than a "place." *It just is.*

I can't report that I saw a white light, nor did I travel down a tunnel according to the classic depiction of a near-death experience (NDE) as defined by Dr. Raymond Moody. All I felt was vast consciousness, and anything that came into my awareness was instantly manifested in front of me. I thought of Asia, for example, and Asia was *in front of me.* I'm not specifically sure why Asia came into my awareness, as I'd never been there; however, it is the best way I can describe how everything was immediately in my realm of awareness, without borders. Even the most remote place I could imagine appeared in my limitless sphere of consciousness.

I was definitely not creating this in my mind, as I was the furthest from analytical thinking I had ever been. I was purely experiencing this peaceful state. I felt so serene and wanted for nothing. There were no unmet needs, hopes, or goals. There were no desires, as everything was present at that moment.

What I would find so interesting when I looked back on it was the absence of pain in that state. What I know now is that all discomfort is created in the mind. I had no feeling of pain after my accident—in fact, I couldn't feel my body at all. Now I see bodies as beautifully intelligent sacs of fluid and bones, encapsulated by the boundaries of our skin. Don't get me wrong, because I love our human bodies and know that they are amazing creations, but I also know for a fact that we are not our bodies. We are pure expanded consciousness.

Back at the mountain, one of the EMTs was asking, "Are you Jon?"

"Yes," a familiar voice said.

"She has been saying your name. She has been asking for you."

I saw this silver cord, luminescent, pure, and bright, attached between Jon and me. It was like a light beam connecting us. I saw the connection, and knew that it was something quite significant.

At that moment, I jumped back into my body, which felt very confined and small. I looked up, and my eyes met Jon's. I didn't have the ability to speak because my body had been throwing up. These wonderful medics kept turning my head to the side so that I wouldn't choke on my own vomit. Even though I couldn't form any words, I marveled that I *could* communicate in a new way.

I spoke from my eyes to his eyes. And it was one of the most powerful and complete communications I had ever experienced.

It only lasted seconds, and then I left again, returning to this beautiful place of expanded consciousness.

That day on the mountainside, I found out that Jon was my soul mate, as that cord was our link. Eventually, we would create an amazing life together and an incredible daughter. As a couple, we have an absolute knowing that this other realm exists. My memory of visiting it is crystal clear, like it just happened yesterday. I could never forget it.

In my research interviewing various guests, I would come to learn that there are dimensions to this vast consciousness. I'd realize that I could be a physical body on the ground and experience looking down at my body in that same exact moment. What I have concluded personally is that those are two different dimensions occurring simultaneously—they're two realities and two levels of consciousness. That means that there are two different Lisas existing in different realities. My consciousness is above and below at the same time.

I also learned that it was entirely possible to go into a meditation and jump into these other quantum realities and co-create a desired outcome or a state of joy or a goal in another reality, knowing full well that it was actually occurring. When I would jump into those different realities, I would create on a totally different level and thus cause my physical neural networks to bundle and group together to form new memories. So, when I'd come back into this daily, waking life, I would have formed a neural bridge that made a memory of where it was that I was going.

Later, I would call this process "remembering your future." I'd do it with my daughter before soccer games or before my own important interviews. Any of us can do it to create a state of change, like going from upset to happiness. There are many different ways to use this shift in consciousness, which I'll discuss in the second part of this book. I can tell you that for me this new consciousness is a work in progress, an experiment, and a whole lot of fun. Wayne Dyer, my friend and mentor, and I have had several enlightening conversations on and off the radio about these various dimensions of consciousness.

You just have to turn up the emotion and create your desired outcome.

ON THAT DAY BACK IN 1999, I discovered that I wanted to live again in my physical body. My work in this dimension wasn't done—and neither was my physical life. I knew that if I returned to living my life, I would try to bring that feeling of expanded consciousness into everything I would do on Earth, including every relationship, every conversation, and every interaction. I would also bring it to every struggle, every elation, and every moment where I would love and be loved.

With my body sprawled out in the pine needles, I heard the fast chugging of a helicopter that landed to airlift me to the hospital. "It's her only chance," one of the EMTs said. "She's dying."

I heard him say something about putting a shot into my arm, and I knew that I didn't want one. I had been a proponent of natural healing my entire life, and I felt that whatever he was going to put in my arm would kill me because I was holding on by a thread. Again I jumped back into my body, knocked his hand away, and somehow motioned, *"No!"* Thinking back, it was probably just a saline solution to rehydrate my body, but I was in survival mode and wasn't thinking clearly at all.

With another great chugging sound, the helicopter took off.

At Henry Mayo Newhall Memorial Hospital, I was stabilized. When I came to, I could see Jon in the corner of my room, and I remember thinking, *I don't know how I got here. How did I get into this room?* As I looked around to try to figure out exactly where I was, I heard the dull voice of a doctor asking, "What is your name? What is your birth date?"

When I opened my mouth, nothing came out.

I knew everything that I wanted to tell him, but I couldn't connect the words and the thoughts to anything that resembled speech. It was as if the words were stuck on lockdown in some sort of mental prison.

The doctor looked at both Jon and me, and I started to panic. *What's wrong with me? Why can't I speak? I spent my entire life as a verbal person, and now I've been silenced.*

The doctor handed me a piece of paper, and I was elated that I could write what was going on in my mind. The first thing I wrote down was my parents' phone number, which was honestly the only thing I could think to do in that moment. It seemed like a good idea because my mom and dad definitely knew my medical history, although they were hours away from this hospital. Jon, my ex, would have to be my voice.

The initial diagnosis was brain damage from hitting my head several times. I was told that my helmet had cracked in 13 places, but "thank God you had a helmet on or you would be dead." The prognosis was murky, as it usually is when it comes to brain injuries.

"We just don't know," the doctor told Jon. "The brain could heal—or not. Time will tell."

My ability to communicate was reduced to grunting, pointing, and writing. It was beyond frustrating to have a thought and not be able to release it from my head. Again, in so many ways I felt like a prisoner. In moments like these, you realize that the ability to speak is one of your greatest blessings along with the ability to think. When either is gone, it's utterly devastating and fills you with feelings of abject fear and utter helplessness.

During my week in the hospital, I did begin to regain my voice, and I was beyond grateful. But I wasn't speaking normally, as my words would slur and my speech was interrupted with noises and grunts.

I was told that I needed to go home and rest my brain: "No physical activity. No reading. Nothing straining. Just rest." I lived alone at the time, and felt a slow panic start to creep in as I realized that I needed care and would probably have to go back to live with my parents. And then Jon suggested that I recover at his house, where it would be peaceful and quiet. I was so thankful and took him up on his generous offer, which was above and beyond the call of duty since we weren't even a couple any longer. At that time, he didn't know what I had experienced on that mountaintop and the silver cord that I saw unite us. In his world, we were a former couple and he was helping an ex-girlfriend get her life back on track.

Once at Jon's house, I was like any patient who was trying to recover. My full vocal powers did return, which was nothing short of a miracle, but I was still slurring my words for weeks after my hospital stay. It would take six long months to be able to speak articulately and with my full, past powers of speech—which, like everyone else, I had absolutely taken for granted. The other scary part was that my short-term memory was completely wiped out, like someone had taken an eraser over the entire chalkboard.

Huge chunks of my past were missing or deleted, and as I tried to find them, I kept coming up with holes.

Friends and family members would tell me stories, and I'd search in my brain for that amazing day at the flower mart that we enjoyed together. There was nothing there. I could only vaguely remember my childhood room. (To this day, I still can't picture any of the details.)

Jon was amazing in that he simply gave me the space to heal. Part of that healing included doing research into *what* heals the brain. Soon I found myself at an EEG center, a place that works with kids and adults suffering from brain injuries, seizures, and ADHD.

At the center, doctors put electrodes on my scalp to show them what areas of my brain were responding. "I'm going to send signals to different parts of your brain," said the technician, who then could show me on a scan what parts weren't coming back strong. In my case, the weak areas were in the prefrontal cortex and in the memory center.

I had a company to run, and I refused to allow myself to accept defeat. As my speech returned back to normal, I began to make business calls, but my short-term memory was just that: a memory. In a matter of minutes, I would forget anything that I said to my clients. When I forced myself to try to remember, it just wasn't there. Like a deleted file on a computer, it was gone.

My mother would call to check on me and remind me of funny things I'd said to her, and I'd laugh. But the truth was I didn't remember that, or a lot of things.

"Mom, I have no recollection of saying that to you," I finally admitted with fear in my voice.

Why couldn't I remember?

✻ ✻ ✻

CHAPTER 3

Healing My Brain

As I was healing, I had a recurring dream: I'd be standing on a platform watching a silver bullet train coming toward me from an unknown place, heading somewhere equally unknown. As the train arrived, it seemed to invite me to come aboard, but it was always in motion. Landing hard, I'd jump onto the train and end up in a control room with audio boards and television monitors.

The main thing I would notice were people sitting in these high-backed swivel chairs. They seemed to be teachers and important scientists or visionary leaders, and they were laughing and having a great time. I could feel their sense of joy in doing something they loved and that they didn't take themselves too seriously despite their levels of success. This was always the essence of the dream. When I would step off the train, I'd look back to see the word *Aware* on the side of it. I knew Spirit was trying to tell me that this was how I was supposed to live my life, but I couldn't figure out exactly what that meant.

My business was in disarray, to the point that I almost lost it. My memory lapses were creating serious issues with clients: I'd have a conversation with someone, and then the next day, I'd call them to cover the same ground. "Lisa, don't you remember? This is exactly what we decided yesterday," the client would say. The truth was I couldn't remember at all. The details floated away like dust. Luckily, my employees took over, realizing that I shouldn't be having deep-dish business conversations due to my memory loss.

Similarly, Jon and I could have a discussion about possibly going out for dinner that night, but afterward, I wouldn't have a clue. It was almost as if we'd never talked about it at all because information that went into my brain left it just as quickly. I tried to take the advice of my doctors, who reminded me that my healing process would be slow.

It was also an emotionally painful one. I'd wake up at dawn and watch Jon leave for work. A good part of my morning was then spent looking through the window at the orange tree in his yard. When that got to be too much, I'd go back to bed and try to sleep. Eventually, I'd go to the living room, where I'd gaze at a lemon tree across the street for long stretches of time. Days morphed into weeks, which grew to months, as time became a blur. Meanwhile, I also experienced blank periods where I couldn't think of much of anything at all.

I wondered if my EEG treatments were actually working or not. Although this form of healing has been used successfully for over 50 years, I still had my doubts. *Will my brain ever heal—can it heal? Or will I remain in this vacant state forever? Is EEG really the answer?*

THE EEG TREATMENTS CONSISTED OF going in for an individual appointment in a room where I would sit in a chair. A certified technician would enter, sit behind me, and put electrodes on my head. The objective was for my brain to give feedback to the computer program based on a rewards feature generated from the program. Biofeedback from my brain would then send a signal through electrical impulses, and the program would read the frequencies as being high or low. This helped the technician identify which areas of my brain were responsive or not.

The goal was for the program to have rewarding images appear on the screen when I was in coherent brain-wave pattern. To stimulate my brain, there'd be constant sensory input in this visual form and also auditory prompts— music would go up and down, as the visuals morphed into new forms. I'd get rewarding beeps for correctly following a visual or auditory pattern, and lack of rewards when I wasn't following correctly.

The ongoing electrical activity of my brain would be picked up in an amplifier and then processed in a computer. The objective was for my brain to get to see its own activity on the computer screen in order to shape behavior to more functional patterns. Based on some assumptions about where good brain function lies, the computer program would process the signal and present it in such a way that I would feel rewarded for movement of brain activity in the preferred direction. It was a sophisticated game of "warmer/colder," effectively.

Certain brain-wave frequencies have been found to play particular roles in brain regulation, so these would be selected by the signal processing and tracked through the training session. The ebb and flow of the size of these signals would reflect the behavior of the neurons in my cortex performing their collective dance, the dance of regulation. The fluctuating signal would then be turned into a visual image that was not only pleasing but engaging as well. It drew me into wanting the process to succeed.

The partial image of a colorful hot-air balloon might appear, for instance. If my brain moved in the direction of a larger signal in the desired frequency range, then more of the vibrant balloon would appear. There was a built-in preference, of course, for seeing the balloon whole. The opposite would occur if I'd get distracted or start to feel anxious, or if for one reason or another rogue brain-wave activity would appear, the residue of my injury.

So my brain was being trained like a muscle to react in a positive way through the feedback loop with the EEG program. The feedback was positive in the psychological sense as well, as I repeatedly got to experience the meeting of goals. To engage my brain, there'd be ongoing sensory stimulation in this form, and what would be seen visually would also be corroborated by the ebb and flow in the volume of the accompanying music. Finally, there'd also be auditory alerts for when specific criteria were being met in the EEG—I'd get encouraging beeps under those circumstances. Such beeps might not appear to be all that rewarding to an outside observer, but they would be to the person undergoing the training process.

Just as in any game, you accept the rules. Beeps are good, so you want them, and when they go missing, you want them back. Eventually, of course, they do come back, and you feel successful because you have the impression— rightly or wrongly—that you had something to do with that success. You have the feeling of taking charge of your own brain, when it is actually a case of the brain taking charge of itself.

The visuals are based on various programs that you or your technician chooses, and a variety is available to suit every style of functioning. Some people need highly activating feedback, while others prefer calmer presentations. The technician works on different parts of the cortex for different purposes, and in that manner the training personalizes on the basis of the characteristics of each nervous system, and also on the basis of the objectives of the training. The program could turn out to be very different depending on whether the primary objective is to reduce anxiety, depression, or stress; or whether the objective is just the enhancement of function, as in improving sleep, sharpening up memory, elevating mood, boosting happiness, and so much more.

In one exercise, for example, I watched a butterfly flying around on a screen. In the beginning, the butterfly moved very slowly, fluttering along and even bouncing off the walls. My brain injury made it difficult to focus on something that simple, but as I relaxed into the exercise, my eyes were able to focus and feed information to my brain. The butterfly began to fly faster, which required a more intense concentration to keep up with this movement. My reward for this focus was a jet stream coming off the butterfly, spilling brilliant stars and bright red hearts in its wake. In the next few seconds, the butterfly soared higher in the sky. As the electrodes attached to my head registered my comprehension, the reward was additional hearts and stars, plus a continuation of the saga.

As my brain continued to slowly recover, I moved past the phase where the butterfly was simply flying around to a new level where quite suddenly a window appeared, followed by a tunnel. As my brain processed these images, the hemisphere between the ocean and the sky was defined, and my reward was the image morphing into the most beautiful sunset. The more my brain was rewarded, the more it desired to stay in a benign state. The feedback made for a direct interaction with my neural networks at an unconscious level, and at the same time engaged my desire for mastery and connected me with my feeling states.

When the brain has faced trauma like my accident, it has a tendency to repeat the same pattern over and over again, refusing to move on. It cannot get out of the bind it's in. Those traumatic neural patterns are solidified in a brain injury, and as self-protection, the brain is inclined to return to painful memories and constantly refresh them. This is what is known as the trauma response.

EEG neurofeedback guided my brain to move out of the patterns in which it had been stuck, which allowed it to move to the next level and not repeat the same memories. My injured brain was being given the opportunity to build new patterns and improve itself. As function was gradually restored, the opportunity to create even better function opened up.

As my brain healed, I returned to a state where the old information or visuals dissipated like normal, where I wasn't repeating the same pattern over and over again. Instead, I built new patterns in my brain so that I could comprehend many things at once.

As I built these new patterns of association, I created the opportunity for healthy habits to be established. Then I was able to layer in intention and goals, and my brain started living within a framework of new memories. In short, I began to visualize new things in order to break old patterns. The recovery process gradually moved from one that was largely unconscious to one that was ever more under my conscious direction, as the basis for my personal autonomy was restored.

Another way to think about it is to imagine that you're raised on $5 a day without enough to eat. You're always in survival mode, and you need to break that pattern by living a new way. It's the same thing with a brain injury where you're also in survival mode, coping with functioning while healing. You need to break out of that pattern of injury, but the brain does not appear to be able to accomplish that by itself.

The reason is paradoxical. The fact is that the injured brain is at every moment still trying its best to function —it is just not succeeding. When the brain continues to strive out of a pattern of dysfunction without success, then it may end up actually exacerbating that dysfunction. Behaviors that are repeated again and again will end up being learned very well, leaving you even more stuck.

The pathway out of this bind is paradoxical as well. It is to guide the brain toward calm states in which it is not striving. The entire process of neurofeedback is oriented to guide the brain toward calm and organized states so that it may learn to live there. It is these calm states out of which function then emerges when the brain faces its challenges. This is the real secret of good brain function. Highly competent brains aren't competent because they're working hard. On the contrary, they are competent because they're at ease.

It was fascinating to learn how my brain worked and to feel the difference when I was in a state of coherence, of complete calm. During the EEG exercise, my brain activity was reflected in the butterfly moving along, and my brain also reacted to that movement. My brain was exercising control over the signal, and was thus relearning *how* to control. And in the process, my brain was moving toward that place of calmness in which it needed to live.

In another version of this kind of training, the scene in front of me was a white sandy beach with gently lapping waves. The intention here was to diminish any sense of striving toward a goal on my part. The real signal was embedded in the size of the image, which varied slowly on the screen. That's what my brain was paying attention to while my conscious self was enjoying the peaceful scene.

In order to reach a truly calm state, it was helpful to eliminate all striving. This was accomplished by distracting my conscious mind with irrelevancies. This was proof at the brain level that our striving self does not help when profound calmness is the objective.

ALL OF THIS MIGHT SOUND SIMPLE—and in practice it is—but at the conceptual level it was hardly simple at all. I was actually taking my brain out of injury mode by calming and de-stressing it, for which the path needed to be found. This is not at all what I thought at the beginning when I entered this process. By these means, I found myself getting back to the level of mental processing and type of thinking that I took for granted before my bike accident.

Even without the impetus of my injury, this would have been a great way to train my mind to avoid distractions. I found this treatment modality to be a crucial part of getting past a traumatic brain injury, and I know it can also help those dealing with emotional reactions regain their mental focus. This method has proven itself to be an effective technique for PTSD and trauma patients.

The EEG treatments also helped me push past the emotional trauma of knowing that my brain was injured. The emotional stress of having a brain injury and wondering if I would ever recover and feel like normal again was overwhelming and confusing at times. Once again, I would learn that not dealing with my emotional stress was actually working against my recovery.

EEG calmed me and helped me know as I progressed that I was indeed getting better, even if the improvement seemed like it was coming at a glacial pace. Instead of living in a state of panic, I replaced it with gratitude because of my good fortune in having found my way to this method. Many candidates for this training never find out about it. One of my doctors recommended it, and it was one of the best tools I had in my long recovery.

I can't say that I always lived in this gratitude, though. There were so many days while my brain was recovering that I felt like a prisoner trapped in my own body and couldn't find my way out. I was miserable, and weeks seemed to pass with what appeared to be very little progress. I continued to forget the words I had just spoken or the plans that I made hours before, which was both humiliating and frightening at the same time. At night, I would remain awake in the dark, staring at the slats in the window blinds, and wonder how I could stop living in fear and get out of my own way.

When I went to my EEG treatments, I found myself in a waiting room with brave children who were there because they were prone to seizures and other brain-related issues. Self-defeating thoughts along the lines of *What am I doing here?* were replaced with the awareness that I was fortunate to be at these treatments, and would somehow use every minute of this technique to rebuild what was temporarily broken.

I STARTED MY EEG TREATMENT with Dr. Barry Sterman, who pioneered some of the very early treatments using electroencephalogram for seizures and strokes. After 12 sessions, there was major retesting to see if I was ready to go to another level. Let me just say that *every* session was a struggle because a damaged brain naturally wants to go to sleep to heal, when it really needs retraining. I did my first round of EEG and felt a slight difference, but I was promised that the rewards don't come right away because the brain doesn't figure things out in a nanosecond; it needs repetition to create a new and lasting pattern.

I didn't get the full hot-air balloon on the screen until the sixth session, and that was a victory because the pieces of the balloon built up as my brain progressed. All in all, this process took a lot of patience and discipline—it took about 20 sessions to see real progress, where I was thinking much more clearly and had dramatically better short-term memory retention.

Although my memory did come back over the next several months, there were still holes in it. The fear lingered longer than the challenge of recovery presented itself. I was afraid that the things I had forgotten would remain that way. When I was reminded of a memory lapse, I was gripped with fear because I felt like I was losing my past. This is why I have the most empathy for senior citizens dealing with memory loss or just the fear of not remembering.

Nevertheless, none of my progress would have been achieved if I stayed in bed, scared, and sleeping the days away. I wasn't going to crawl under the covers and give up, because I vowed to be proactive. I was retraining my brain doing what I call "brain-nastics." Yes, it was like gymnastics for the brain!

It also proved to me beyond a shadow of a doubt that our anxiety and other negative emotions truly do hurt us physically by preventing our functioning optimally. In fact, I later learned that business CEOs and top athletes use EEG training all the time to motivate them and to work on personal development and goals. It's about training the brain for intentional thinking.

I was told during my EEG training that meditation was a key part of my recovery. Meditation can also be a very effective way to achieve total brain coherence and a state of flow. I found that EEG actually made it easier to flow into a meditative state as I was now accustomed to focusing in this way.

In addition to EEG, here's something you can do very simply right now to bring your brain into a relaxed state. It's a technique I learned from Dawson Church, a researcher of evidence-based psychological and medical techniques: Just relax your tongue and let it fall to the bottom of your mouth. That simple act puts your brain into a meditative state. Stop. Enjoy this moment and think of positive images. You will find it hard to be negative in this state because your brain wants to relax. You can use this technique anywhere, and it's especially helpful during times of stress.

Today I am still doing neurofeedback sessions to continue to train my brain at the EEG Institute in Woodland Hills, California, operated by Dr. Siegfried Othmer and his wife, Dr. Susan Othmer (www.EEGinstitute.com). I find these sessions most valuable to remain healthy.

I will always keep EEG sessions as a part of my routine to stay focused, sleep well, and maintain a strong immune system; I have even found it effective for balancing my hormones. EEG neurofeedback can also be used for peak performance, enhancing concentration, treating migraines, removing addictions, relieving depression and anxiety, and so many more things that are not related to a traumatic brain injury. It's an incredible healing modality, and I'd encourage anyone to explore it if they're interested.

* * *

CHAPTER 4

Healing My Body

To my great relief, my brain was healing. However, each day seemed to bring challenges with my memory, as well as persistent fears that I had to push past in order to relax into my recovery. At the same time, I was told that keeping my body in top shape was crucial during this time. The old slogan, "A healthy body and a healthy mind go hand in hand" was never more apparent to me. As soon as my physicians gave me the all clear to add physical activity to my life, the question became: *what* physical activity? As someone who had always been super active in her life, I was a bit worried about what I would do to get back in optimal shape again. Would it involve something on two wheels?

After months of staring at Jon's orange tree in his backyard, I knew that I had to jolt myself out of my depression. The simple act of getting out of bed in the morning was the first step, and it was a crucial one because it's so easy to stay under the covers while recovering from anything, including depression or a serious illness. And then one day, I went outside and got right back in the saddle. I simply took a long, slow ride around the block on a mountain bike, and it felt so good to move again.

I knew that getting my blood flowing would help my body recover. I could ride outside or use the stationary bike that Jon kept in the house—there were no excuses. I began to get out of bed every single day, even when I had little sleep or went to bed past midnight, and exercised. I would push myself out of bed even on those mornings when I barely knew my own name or what I had planned to do. I didn't remember much except that I needed to physically move to recover my mind, body, and spirit. There was just no other choice.

I have always been someone who basically can't function until I get at least 30 to 60 minutes of exercise every day. Even when I'd go out of town before the accident and had very little time to work out, I'd still go for a power walk or even do the hotel stairs for 15 to 20 minutes. Now as I recovered, I'd combine the bike with some of my favorite floor exercises, including sit-ups, push-ups, high knees, and dips off of the bed. I can't even tell you how good it felt to sweat; sweating is a great form of detoxification. Everyone self-regulates in a different way, and moving my blood helps me wake up and ramp up.

DURING MY HEALING, I KNEW IT WAS IMPORTANT for me both mentally and physically to start mountain biking again. Jon was still doing three- or four-hour rides, and I was definitely unable to handle that pace. That doesn't mean that I just sat it out; instead, I did what I could do. The crucial part of this was that I tried to do as much as possible, and didn't give that old excuse of "someday I'll try it again."

Although I know he's had his own issues, I did read Lance Armstrong's book *It's Not About the Bike* at the time, and admired how he healed from cancer after treatments and from sheer determination. It was so admirable to me that while he was recovering from the devastating effects of chemotherapy, he would drag himself out of the bed and get on the stationary bike that he had set up in his hospital room. Between rounds of chemo, he would sit on that bike and pedal super slowly. You could say that I identified because that's exactly what I was doing as I healed from my brain injury. Biking and EEG were the two activities that truly made me feel better as they pushed me to embrace the hope that I would make a full recovery.

When I biked outside, it was on flat ground, and I'd pedal while thinking about the accident that left me in this state. Doctors told me that despite the fact that I did drink the recommended amount of water on the day of the almost-fatal race, the heat was too much and left my body dehydrated. Knowing why helped the pieces of the puzzle fall into place.

It was meditative for me to get on that bike again with my new helmet and go for a ride outside where the breeze felt so good on my face. Gradually, I left the pavement and reveled in the sound the rocks and dirt made crunching under my wheels. It was therapy for me to be in the dirt again without the threat of cars whizzing by too close. I biked to a chorus of birds singing, and my companions were the lizards that would scurry out of my way or the occasional snake that would move a few protesting inches to avoid the threat of my tires.

I've always been told that being out in nature is healing as you absorb the powerful energy of the earth, and I found this to be especially true for me. I biked on what I called healing ground.

I came to find that exercise heals in so many ways. This explains why cyclists are so addicted to the bike and runners are equally passionate about hitting the pavement.

I can't state this enough: Being in good shape before my accident put me so much ahead of the healing curve than I would have been if I hadn't worked out. That alone should be inspiration for all of us to get to the gym on those days when we really don't feel like it.

ALMOST 11 MONTHS POST-ACCIDENT, Jon and I had a little talk. "Why not go back into racing again, and finish it?" he asked. "Win the series!" I knew he had a point. I started riding with him, and it wasn't long before I was going for an hour without even knowing it. It took two months of slow, long-distance rides with him before I could do a ride with 20 or 30 people. I found that the rides gave me energy instead of exhausting me, and I loved to be outdoors, feeling sweaty and alive.

In 1999, I was second in the state. Now Jon gave me that careful little push to get back into the game. "This is something you will hold on to for the rest of your life if you don't get back on that bike and race again," he told me.

One year later, I won the California State Mountain Biking Championship. It was equally healing, not to mention just plain cool, to know in my heart and soul that I was a state champion. Believe me when I say that this was a big hurdle in my life, and something that I needed to prove to myself as a personal victory. It was on that same trail that almost killed me, but I was able to dismiss any frightening flashbacks and concentrate on the here and now.

And I won—in more ways than I could have ever imagined! It was my own personal best that I was going for, along with the idea of knowing that the mountain didn't conquer me. Instead, *I* conquered the mountain, as well as my fear of returning to the scene of the accident.

To this day, if I ever find myself near Castaic Lake, as I did recently driving my daughter to a soccer game, my heart rate still raises and the cellular memory returns of my devastating accident. However, I am so grateful that the memory I now have is that of accomplishment, rather than defeat and regret that I didn't go back and confront that fear.

I got to wear the California State Champion jersey, which I still have (along with the ripped jersey from my accident that had to be cut off of me in the emergency room). But this didn't have anything to do with who was in first or second place. My race was against myself, and it was for a prize I would cherish forever: a more aware life.

* * *

CHAPTER 5

Healing My Life

As I went through the healing process, one question nagged at me: *What type of person do I want to evolve into being?* Would I go back to my usual workaholic self who treated relationships as second priorities after that last phone call of the day (and then the one after that), or had I truly changed?

This was one of the most difficult periods in my life because I've always been such a high-performance person. I knew that I wanted to keep my business, which meant a lot to me, but I also did some deep soul-searching and discovered that work wasn't everything. Jon was so patient, kind, and loving to me that it became obvious that this relationship meant more to me than anything else in my life. But how could I tell him? And would he still be in love with someone who wasn't whole yet?

There was no denying that I had found someone who was not only protective, smart, and loyal, but just a truly great guy. How many other former boyfriends would take an ex in during the hardest time of her life, when her head clearly wasn't on straight, and open his home to her needs? But could he open his *heart* to me again?

Jon was quite clear in telling me that he wasn't willing to jump right in and take me back as his partner in the true sense of the word. This was real life, not a movie where the happy ending occurred after the medical miracle. Instead, he let me know that while he still had feelings for me, he was also very hurt. I'm the first one to say that I wasn't emotionally present before the accident. In the past, I acted out from childhood issues stemming from a father who was often absent. As a young woman, I didn't have men high on my list of priorities, as they were creatures I approached with caution. Of course, I did long for true love . . . someday.

Before the accident, I worked so hard that I frequently slept at the office. What was the point of driving home? This might have been great for my business, but it was not so good for my love life. I didn't know the real Lisa before my accident, but I had met her during my recovery, and I liked this new person who was living a purposeful life instead of a reactionary one.

"I've changed now," I repeatedly told Jon, but the words weren't enough for either of us.

"I need time," he said, making it clear that I would be given an opportunity to prove how I had changed. As I healed, though, it seemed like he kept waiting for the old me to kick back in.

It was obvious that we had deep feelings for each other, but we were both afraid to take that next step. "How long is it going to be before you let me back in again?" I finally asked him one cool night, as we sat in his yard after dinner.

"Lisa, just keep doing what you're doing, which is being present and emotionally there, and not singularly focused on business," he replied. "You can say you've changed, but I have to see it through your actions and not your words."

I knew he had a point and had to protect his own heart from being hurt again. But I was so sad that he couldn't see what I felt, which was a seismic internal shift. I wanted to shout that I couldn't go back to my old ways. In fact, I couldn't even *remember* some of my old ways.

I had a new level of consciousness, awareness, and dimension that showed me a much bigger life picture, and there was no reason to go back. My NDE had taught me that there was so much more to life than what I saw right in front of me. I learned that as incredible as the body is, it is made up of skin and bones that simply confine us. Our spirit is so far beyond this physical shell that we have to experience each day here. My accident taught me the key to life: There is no such thing as a dead-end street, but actually a limitless universe to experience if you are truly conscious.

Thanks to the time I spent with Jon post-accident, there was no way I could focus on anything superficial including if I got this client or that job. That's shallow living. I knew that my life needed to have deep meaning both personally and professionally, and the professional part could wait until I got my personal life sorted out. Yes, I have always been a driven person; however, I needed to find a new way of being driven that was focused on a *purpose*.

I knew now that there was so much more to the world than working 15 hours a day. With Jon, I found the first guy who made me want to turn off the business side of myself and really fight for the relationship by giving it the time and emotional bandwidth he—no, we—deserved.

I just had to trust that we would get there at some point.

TWO YEARS AFTER MY ACCIDENT, I wasn't 100 percent sure if Jon had taken me back into his heart. I was still wondering when he asked me to go to Hawaii with him for a vacation.

With those warm tropical breezes and gently swaying palm trees, it was the dream romantic trip, and I had high hopes that he might pop the question. Yet as days passed and we enjoyed the islands, there was no appearance put in by a little box or ring. My heart began to sink because I was so sure we were finally on the same page, and that included a formal commitment.

A week into the trip, Jon suggested that we drive to Hanalei Bay to watch the sun go down. Hawaiian sunsets are spectacular shows where the orange glow of the sun reflecting off the turquoise water makes it appear as if you truly are in heaven. On the way to the bay, I suddenly became hungry and didn't understand why I had to rush to get a milkshake and get back in the car.

"We can't miss the sunset," he insisted. I nearly dropped that shake when he sped off, driving like crazy until he found the perfect spot on the beach. "Let's take a nice walk," he suggested.

Jon proposed just as the sun hit the water, when the sky was a wild tapestry of colors.

The timing was perfect because I had let go of all my baggage and acting out. Relationship issues were gone and priorities were straight. All the games I was running as a lost woman in the world were done, and I was ready to be a true partner.

JON AND I DIDN'T ACTUALLY tie the knot in Hawaii. Instead, we got married in Topanga Canyon, California, at a serene space called the Inn of the Seventh Ray. That week was particularly rainy, and I was like any new bride who thought it certainly would *never* rain on her wedding day. Well . . .

On the day of our wedding, it rained cats, dogs, and every other animal on the planet, and the water poured down at an inch and a half per hour. It was literally a monsoon, but when you're a bride whose brain had returned to an even better state of normal and you're marrying the soul mate of your dreams, you don't allow a little water to rattle you—even when you have hair that tends to get a bit frizzy in overly moist outdoor situations.

We had tarps to cover everyone at the ceremony, but the rain was pounding with such ferocity that no one could hear the vows or the priest. And then we heard a crashing sound, and the tarp above us suddenly burst from the torrents overhead. In the end, everybody got soaked, including Jon and me. But we said those vows that we'd so proudly written ourselves, and laughed at the sheer joy of it all as we said, "I do." By this time my dress was so heavy from the wet fabric that I kept tripping on it.

"Jon, no one will ever forget this wedding," I assured him with a laugh, as a rainbow burst into the sky.

Afterward, we got in our limo for a drive down the coast. As the miles passed, the rain stopped, and it was nothing but blue skies and lots of sun ahead—hopefully a metaphor for where we were heading in life. There was more good news: my hair didn't move because I had so many products in it! By then we were so wet and cold in the limo that we decided to stop at Starbucks for some hot coffee. The local barista gave us our drinks for free because he felt so bad for us.

Once we got to the reception, things just became comical. At one point, someone spilled a whole glass of champagne on my brother's tux, but you couldn't even see it because he was so wet. I remember sitting at our bridal table and the waterfall next to us was overflowing to the point that as we were sitting there, a frog jumped out onto our table.

So, basically it was one of those fancy fish dinners with frogs jumping all over the place. Jon and I were told that water was a blessing of good fortune, so I was happy to invite a few more frogs to party and dance.

I wasn't upset for a minute because I knew this was a sign of how my new husband and I would live our lives together: working hard and playing hard! And by the way, when we go back to the Inn of the Seventh Ray, I smile when I hear that people are *still* talking about our wedding.

Three months after we got hitched, I found out that I was pregnant. We had our daughter, Kayla, in 2002, and that time was pretty crazy when it came to getting my life in order. I was married with a baby and a new home— I had a very full life, which was absolutely fine with me.

I didn't tell Jon about the silver cord I'd seen connecting us until many years later. I wasn't entirely clear about what had happened to me on the mountain until I was attending the University of Philosophical Research, pursuing my master's degree in transformational psychology. (They had given me an honorary bachelor's degree so that I could continue on with my advanced studies.)

One of my professors was Dr. Raymond Moody, who had written the best-selling book *Life After Life*. After reading Dr. Moody's definitions of a near-death experience, a flood of memories came rushing in of the blissful experience I had after the accident.

One of my assignments was to write a paper on my experience, and it was then that I recognized what I had been through. One of the classic symptoms of a NDE is that people tend to discount it, deny it, or forget about it because they can't make sense of it. To this day I am still discovering the language to describe my experience, and the best way to remember is by interviewing others with near-death experiences. It's like we are speaking our own language when we talk.

When I finally told Jon about the silver cord I'd seen, he was touched. That cord is an unbreakable bond between us.

DURING THAT TIME WHEN I WAS RECOVERING from the brain trauma, I was also struggling with what to do professionally. My business was surviving, although it was hard to hear clients say that I was lying because I thought I'd called them back and I hadn't. The entertainment industry doesn't exactly have patience when you're injured, demanding your full attention 24/7. As time progressed, and I got my life in order, I didn't want to live that 24/7 type of work life any longer. My priorities had definitely shifted.

I kept thinking about my recurring dream of the bullet train. The most memorable part to me was the people sitting in front of the audio boards in high-backed swivel chairs laughing and having a great time, and I soon put together that these were new-thought leaders and pioneers of the consciousness movement working with a total sense of joy.

I remembered a sentence that came through every time I had this dream: "Communicating messages that inspire positive growth and change." I decided that this was a direct download from Spirit or whatever dimension was attempting to communicate with me because the message was so clear and it made an indelible imprint on my mind.

One morning, I woke up suddenly and said to myself out loud, "You have to do this."

As soon as I'd made this realization, a friend told me, "There is a personal-development radio station on AM that was just bought out by a Korean company. They're looking to fill an hour or two during the transition."

That's a great way to have a voice, I thought.

At the time, I had a fabulous acupuncturist who was working to help make me healthy again, and I had another friend whose life mission was to cure cancer. I was also speaking to a spiritual leader about my life as I tried to find balance. I thought, *Why not create a conversation with these people about life and their teachings . . . and why not do it on the radio?* I knew this was a way to bring the remarkable work of individuals like this to anyone who just tuned in on the dial.

Of course, I said a resounding yes to the radio show and soon had a time slot. I called it *The Aware Show* because of the name on the train in my dream.

I started my new career in this beautiful high-rise business building in Los Angeles where I'd sit in a small studio and talk about consciousness into a microphone. I discussed issues of awareness with amazing guests who were considered visionaries in their fields of study. It struck me that there weren't enough hours on the radio to bring their life-changing work to a listening base that was growing by leaps and bounds each week.

Eventually, the owners of my small radio show went through one of those media mergers, which I knew meant it was time for me to pitch my show to various other stations. *The Aware Show* was quickly picked up by KPFK, a political talk-radio/public-radio station.

It wasn't long before my endless fascination with the brain came to the airwaves on my show. I wanted to know more about how it functions when it's damaged, so with a series of different experts, I explored why the brain does what it does and how neurons connect and create patterns or havoc. I knew that it's hard to do anything or even be yourself if your brain is injured. I also realized that the average person didn't need to suffer a head trauma in order to experience some sort of brain damage.

Our modern lives are filled with stress, trauma, and unresolved emotional tragedies; these alone or in combination create quite the "head trip." In fact, so many of us are addicted to stress, which then makes our cortisol levels rise, as well as those of other stress hormones. Whether we're injured or not, we're actually hooked on the rush of our cortisol levels rising. And the purpose of adrenaline is to help us deal with "flight or fight" survival issues, which is what humans faced during primitive times—yet we now live in a state where our adrenaline pumps almost constantly.

I was still experiencing my own healing, and there were times when I had to close my eyes and really focus. Even so, I found that being on the radio every day was actually quite healing for me because my brain was in constant training. I did my show with focus and intention, while also committing to the idea that I could help others heal their own lives and become more aware on a daily basis. Soon, I found that doing the show even increased my energy levels and brought me into a different state of consciousness. I believe this is why the show has done so well, because to this day it brings a healing energy to me, and this energy translates to anyone who listens.

I have found that my personal formula for success is being of contribution to others while expressing my own passion and mission in life. I see this all the time with the authors and experts I interview. Whenever their body of work is birthed out of their story and deep experiences, they are always successful. That is how I determine who will be a good person to interview—their story is the catalyst for their accomplishment.

When people ask how I was able to get to such a successful point myself, my answer is simple: With the help of incredible specialists, I healed my brain. And with the help of a talented production team, we produce great radio. My career stems from a desire to help people first and foremost, which in turn helps *me* every day. I can be having the worst day, and the minute I sit down to do an interview, my whole world stops. I listen intently, and sometimes it's the only time of day that I just focus on one thing.

I realize how far I've come from my own prison of not being able to speak after my accident to now speaking on the public airwaves. It had been terrifying to be trapped within my own body and brain where nobody could help me get out. Psychiatrist Dr. Daniel Amen says, "If you don't use it, you'll lose it," when it comes to the brain. Now I'm using mine on the radio in a major way. I'm continuing my brain-nastics!

My LIFE HAS ALSO COME FULL CIRCLE. When our beautiful daughter, Kayla, was five, Jon and I took her back to the scene of my accident, where we experienced the mountain as a family. Standing there holding my little girl, I looked at the trail that I crashed on—a single track on a long hill that led to the top of a jagged ridge—and I let myself absorb how far I had come in my life. Gazing at the pine trees in the distance on another hot day, I knew that I'd almost died in that spot. But now I needed to let it go.

I took a well-deserved moment to realize that *I* could conquer the worst-case scenario and not allow it to conquer me. That moment was very symbolic in my life, or should I say on this wild ride called human existence.

I recognized that I was indeed a blessed woman to have healed, found love, and then discovered a calling on the radio.

Now, in the next part of the book, I'd like to share with you some helpful tips I picked up along the way. You too can attain the aware life I have worked so hard to have!

* * *

Part II

Living an Aware Life

CHAPTER 6

Aware of Manifesting What You Want

One of my all-time favorite sayings is, "Where there's a will, there is *definitely* a way." It's not that I'm such an optimistic person that I throw caution to the wind and hope for the best possible results. I truly do believe that your thoughts and intentions create your reality, so my life is based on creating what I want in life on multiple levels.

It's actually quite easy, inspiring, and results-driven to live in this way instead of feeling like we're victims of what's going on around us. The truth is that we're powerful beings who were put here to live very fruitful lives. Quite often what stops us is . . . us. That's why I wanted to start this section of the book by cracking the code for you when it comes to living a life with awareness.

Remember these words:

Think about what you want.
Create it in your mind.
Become it with enthusiasm.
Be grateful for it.

It's just that easy. When you allow the words above to guide you, then you're living in a very positive way—you become who you want to be and get what you want. This is the law of vibrational attraction, and if you focus on this sort of living, you can become one of those people who easily draws to you so many wonderful opportunities.

Why It Works

Let's start with an example from a couple who called in to my radio show one day. Both Bill and Janet faced job layoffs in a tough economy: he was a reporter whose newspaper had suffered severe cutbacks, and she worked at the local school district and felt the pain when one-third of the staff was fired because of budget cuts in the community. They had a bit of savings to live on, but worried that the money wouldn't go far in taking care of both of them and their two young sons. Each day when the mail arrived, Bill would curse the bills that were pouring in.

As they looked for new employment, they had their little freak-out moments. Bill talked about how much it upset him when Janet spent too much money on groceries and the occasional clothing purchase; Janet would rant and rave about how Bill should have gotten out of the publishing industry years ago. They were playing the blame game, which wasn't just hurting their marriage, but also turning their home into a major stress zone for their entire family.

I know a lot of people like this couple who are struggling financially, and I can tell you that the worst thing you can do when money is tight is to focus on what creates even more fear. Freaking out over bills or blaming a once-powerful wage earner only serves to foster negative feelings. If you wake up at three in the morning worried that soon you'll be homeless or that the electricity will be turned off, you might actually contribute to making that doomsday prediction come true.

When you're aware, though, you look at this situation in a completely different way. You take action and don't just sit on the couch wishing for something good to happen.

> ## AWARISM
> Awareness plus action is the perfect combination
> for having the life you want to live.

Yes, it's a shame that Bill and Janet lost their jobs around the same time. No, there was nothing that could have been done because both were hard workers who were facing tough economic times. Yes, both were diligently looking for new employment, which was crucial. I told these two to stop yelling and blaming, and calmly come together and fix the problem. I mentioned to them that a good place to start was to sit down and visualize individually what they want.

The next step was to ask each other what it would feel like to have the kind of financial freedom to do what they wanted to do. I let them know that seeing, hearing, tasting, smelling, and feeling something in the most real way they could would be the quickest avenue to creating it.

They needed to imagine it using all five senses, and turn up the emotions. Then they needed to take action and *do* something concrete toward whatever it was that they visualized.

AWARISM

Visualizing where you want to be using all five senses is the key to creating the life you desire, even if it's the last thing you want to do. Sure, it's easier to feel sorry for yourself and feel depressed. Instead, take on the challenge to keep looping positive visualizations through your mind's eye until it literally creates a neural bridge in your mind and becomes a memory.

If you're in the same boat as Bill and Janet, you might not find full-time employment right away, but you can find a part-time or even a volunteer job in the field you have always wanted to be in. You must make a very real "play" to create where you want to be in life. Note that you want to create from a place of calmness and freedom rather than one of, "We're going to lose the house!"

You don't want to say to yourself in fear, "What am I going to do?" You want to calm down and say, "This is where I need to be. This is what I'm going to do to get there. My first step will be attending that financial conference on June 1 where I'll submit an application to five new companies. I'll get in that paperwork by Friday to help me secure the interim cash to give me the time to start my business. I can even turn my hobby into a side job by creating an online business to carry me over."

In this way, you are working to create a more positive and powerful path forward.

Remembering Your Future:
The Key to Awareness

Earlier in the book, I mentioned a process I call "remembering your future," and I have found that it is key to living an aware life. In your mind, you experience what it feels like to live the life that you want and make note of how it feels to live a specific dream. Remember that in the future, what you want actually exists, and you don't need a near-death experience like my own to see what is ahead of you. You can sit down in any quiet space and create memories in the future.

Neuroscience studies show that when the brain travels into a visualization in the future, it will work toward getting exactly what you want. That's because you're forming new neural pathways and bundles of the images you want to achieve as if they are already happening. What we want is highly individual. Perhaps you want to have the ideal house, a wonderful relationship, or enough money saved to retire early. Maybe you just want to get through the next few difficult days with your family. Your future could be five years or five minutes from now.

So many times, my executive producer and friend, Gina Salvati, and I have looked at each other in a knowing way while one of us said, "This moment, right now, is exactly what we created in our visualization of the future." When we would travel together, we'd sit on the airplane and visualize where we wanted to see *The Aware Show* go and how it would help people heal. We co-created the future of the show through many of these visualizations.

Again, this works because visualization creates the neural bridges and synapses to make it happen. Dr. Joe Dispenza demonstrates this in his fascinating videos of neurons firing and wiring together in the brain. And in his book *Breaking the Habit of Being Yourself,* he says, "The latest research supports the notion that we have a natural ability to change the brain and the body by thought alone."

Think of it this way: When you have a thought, it triggers the release of a chemical neurotransmitter that then drifts across the gap between two neurons. When it reaches the other side, it fits into a special receptor of the target neuron, like a key in a lock. When you visualize in this way, you create the synapses that dictate future events. You're building the neural bundles in your brain as you create the memory in the future. When you get there and are in fact living that life, you can rejoice at how you created this event.

For example, I have always wanted to write a best-selling book. Instead of sitting around wondering if *Becoming Aware* will help as many people as possible, I go into my own future mentally and see letters and e-mails from individuals who changed their life in a significant way as a result of something they read in my book or heard on one of my shows. In feeling my own future, I'm not just living a fantasy, but also creating a neural network in my mind that in reality will form and help me achieve that very result.

This is a very easy exercise in that all you need to do is put a picture up of what you want in your mind's eye. You can also think of your mind like a movie theater, and you're simply hitting "play" on the projector that is showing your future. As you see what you want, you go on a timeline into your future while you continue to create what you want in life.

Let's say that you would like to see $250,000 in the bank by December 15. Put the picture of that number showing up on your bank statement into your mind's eye and attach the future timeline to it. Infuse your energy and breath into that picture while also focusing on that specific date.

You see that $250,000 in the bank ready to invest in your business, or whatever dream you are pursuing, by December 15. Dissolve down into that date and look around and see all of the events and miraculous and fabulous things that will happen as a result of having that money. Let your mind go at this point and allow ideas to flow to you. Think of the people you'll meet through your new business, as well as the philosophy of how you will run that business. See the countless individuals whom you will impact with your work, which is the result of this money. What will your family's future look like because of it? See the date again and continue to peer ahead in time. It's so important that you stop seeing yourself as broke and struggling, and instead see yourself living in that happy, financially sound future.

Remember that your brain is an intense organ in terms of your emotions, and you have five senses to help you experience life. When it comes to seeing into your future, you must use all five of those senses. Ask yourself:

* What does your future *look* like?
* What does your future *feel* like?
* What does your future *smell* like?
* What does your future *taste* like?
* What does your future *sound* like?

Turn up the intensity on all of your senses as you mentally enhance your positive future. As you do, you'll be creating networks in your brain that will make those memories in the future.

In the process, chemicals including dopamine and serotonin will also be released, which will allow you to stay in a happy mood and in a good state. You'll be breaking up old neural patterns and creating new ones. Let's face it —most of us could use a few new neurons!

AWARISM

A positive mind will give you a positive life.

On my radio show, I have heard from many people who have been trying to manifest love in their lives. They tell me that they simply can't find the right person. Of course, I've had many girlfriends who face what they call an "impossible" dating market and worry that they're going to spend the rest of their lives alone. You can't live in fear when it comes to finding new love. Instead, you can use the "remembering your future" technique here to attract love into your life.

In your visualization, it's helpful to actually go into the future and see exactly what you're doing with your new love. Perhaps you're on a beautiful hiking trail on a warm summer morning, just enjoying the day together. Again, what does that feel like for you? What does it look like? What does that morning air smell like? What does it taste like? What are the two of you saying to each other?

Go through all of the senses and decide what this person looks, smells, and feels like, and then slowly experience each of those sensations in your mind. Take your time—this isn't a race, and you have as long as you need.

Think about that hike and the great conversation that you're having on the trail. Feel the connection between the two of you, as it's not forced but is naturally just there. Enjoy the feeling that you're growing with this other person as you both have developed a deep understanding of each other. You want to go on more adventures together and grow old with each other.

Go into that visualization several times a week—as you're falling asleep, sitting in the car in traffic, or soaking in the tub. As you experience the value of that love as if it has happened, you will become that energy and attract it into your life. Then go sign up for a hiking club or a beach clean-up organization for fun.

This is much better than reaching for a box of cookies and moaning about how you can't find love. Your future self who is in love with that amazing man or woman doesn't need an extra-large tub of buttered popcorn because you don't medicate yourself that way. You want fewer love handles as you plunge into your happy future. You don't want the instant gratification of food now for comfort, as you find comfort in the fact that this future love *is* in your future. (Also, keep in mind that you are the only person who can make you happy.)

It's easy to satisfy your body with food when you're feeling sad or uncomfortable. If you eat like you're living your future dream life, then you won't want to consume extra calories.

Picture how you will look in that future and you can easily avoid gaining weight. See your healthy, lean body and face. Now, add to your life a daily yoga or spinning class as a proactive way to make this happen. If you're hungry, exercise and drink plenty of water before you consume unwanted calories. Get that haircut of your future. Buy that pretty dress or nice suit.

Expand your life as you move toward your visualization of the future. One of the biggest missing gaps between a healthy diet plan and actually executing the plan is visualization and accountability. If you connect deeply enough to your desired outcome, then you are more likely to achieve it, rather than going into denial when you reach for unhealthy food.

You need a bigger *why,* and visualization helps you achieve it. If it helps, keep a food journal or sign up for one of the online programs or apps that help keep you accountable with your food.

Taking Action

Visualization alone will not get you to the future that you want to live. It's not enough to just see it; you have to be proactive about it, too. If you desire money, get out there and work toward it. If you're looking for love, then go to the gym so that you'll be the healthiest you possible and have the energy for a new relationship. Work on yourself as your future approaches, as you'll have to launch action toward your goals. If you simply want a more blissful, stress-free life, then take meditation and personal-development classes. The point is that you need to put your future into motion while you're still living in the present.

I look at my own father, who was facing retirement at age 65. He saw his future as a time where he didn't have to be on call 24 hours a day and work so hard, but he also wanted to remain active mentally and physically. Dad had

The hospital band I was given after the accident.

This is the jersey I was wearing the day of the accident—it had to be cut in half in the emergency room.

My California State Mountain Biking Championship kit, which I won in 2000.

Here's a close-up of the jersey.

Family healing in Bali.

Here I am with Anita Moorjani.

With David Wolfe.

An action shot of me interviewing David.

With my friend and mentor, Wayne Dyer.

With Bruce Lipton.

With Deepak Chopra.

Here's Aunt Teri with Jon and new
baby Kayla.

With mermaid Doreen Virtue.

Here I am at the park—being out in nature
is one of my very favorite things.

Triumphantly back on the bike . . . yes!

Biking is one of my favorite things, especially when I get to be in a place as beautiful as Malibu.

a hard time with suddenly stopping being an orthopedic surgeon because his mind was still active and curious. In his vision, he saw a retirement where his mind remained as sharp. But instead of just envisioning it, he shocked everyone when he signed up for a comedy class. His next step was an astronomy course and then a meditation seminar.

Now he's 75 years old and living the future of his vision where he has varied interests and his mind is stimulated. He's a wonderful example of how vision and action work together toward a goal.

A Story Set in the Future

Recently, I went to Colorado to do a series of recordings with other Hay House authors at an I Can Do It! conference. After hours of recording one day, we went to see Wayne Dyer speak in the evening, which was amazing.

Wayne introduced me to Anita Moorjani, author of *Dying to Be Me*. In 2006, Anita had been in a coma for 30 hours due to the fact that she had end-of-life cancer, and the doctors said that her organs were failing. In her state of altered consciousness, she connected with Divine Source.

When she told me about her trip to the Other Side, it was like speaking with someone in a special language— we both knew that this was where all things were created, all things are, and all things exist. It wasn't just validating for both of us; it was also wonderful for her to express some of the same feelings I knew to be true from my own near-death experience.

Anita put into words the immense feeling of love and compassion she experienced in this state, which were the two most memorable feelings I had as well. She explained it as the most pure form of joy she had ever experienced, and her memory of it was still crystal clear, as if it had just happened.

Anita told me that she had seen herself being operated on from above her body and heard the conversations the doctors had as they were working on her. The remarkable thing here is that she could hear them even when they were not in the same room with her, as she would later find out.

She also felt the hopelessness that her beloved husband, Danny, was experiencing. Even so, she decided to leave him for a time to explore this new realm—and she found her late father, who now resided in this beautiful, clear place of consciousness.

Anita and her father talked about her difficult past, including how she had walked away from an arranged marriage. She had been ostracized in her Indian community and went on to marry Danny, a man she fell in love with, rather than the one who had been chosen for her by others. She now understood that every encounter and event was woven together to create the fabric of her life, and she found that she only needed to forgive herself.

She came to realize that we are not our bodies; rather, our bodies are simply the shells that we are forced to live in, and they are only a reflection of our inner state. Yes, they are intelligent shells, but she realized how limiting they truly are. Anita understood that she was pure love, just as everyone is, and that if she released fear and allowed herself to be the love she truly was, she would heal herself. In other words, if her external body reflected her internal state, she would have a *completely healthy* body.

That's exactly what happened. Anita's cancer is currently in remission.

You Can Choose a Different State

One of the more frightening times of my life happened quite suddenly one day when I was sitting at my desk after a conference call with my *Aware Show* team. It was one of our typical planning sessions and certainly nothing out of the ordinary; we are always looking at scheduling, outlining future projects, and staying on top of current ones.

I felt the right side of my face freeze and start to solidify to the point where I could not move it. When I tried to talk, I slurred my words because I couldn't lift the right side of my lip. When I smiled, the right side of my face would not rise. I started to panic, but I also knew that I had no time to waste. Immediately, I went into action and called every doctor and practitioner I knew to ask if they had any idea what was going on. My alternative dentist, Dr. Alireza Panahpour, diagnosed me as having Bell's palsy, which is the sudden paralysis of the facial nerve. He said to come in immediately, although his office was a 45-minute drive away!

I jumped in my car and got on the crowded freeway. As I inched my way through traffic, I tried to remember to breathe. This was one of the moments when I needed to use every tool I had learned to stay calm. The more I panicked, the more I thought my face would freeze. Of course I had thoughts that my face would permanently stay this way, but I wouldn't allow those thoughts to linger for very long.

I learned a technique called "four square breathing" from a Pranic Healing Master, Stephen Co. I did this all the way to the dentist's office by imagining a square: I would breathe in for a count of four while drawing one side of the square with my finger in the air, hold the breath for another count of four while drawing the next side of the square, breathe out another count of four while drawing the third side of the square, and hold for the last count of four while completing the square with my finger in the air. Then I would repeat. This technique has been known to lower blood pressure, stress, and anxiety—believe me when I tell you that it really works.

When I arrived at his office, Dr. Panahpour took one look at me and began treatment. He said that the most important thing I could do was to relax and not panic because the treatment was going to work better that way. I had to believe I was going to be fine and not let the default mechanism of negative thoughts flood in.

Tears streamed down my face, which was more of a release of fear for me. My spiritual teacher Michael Tamura taught me that tears are a release of energy that allows the letting-go process to begin, so my tears actually allowed me to calm down and get a hold of my thoughts. I sat back in the dentist chair, closed my eyes, and began to visualize my face returning to normal—all of the feeling coming back in full and smiling again.

For several weeks, I continued on my path of going to neurologists and specialists to help regain the feeling and restore the drooping in my face. A high percentage of people fully recover from Bell's palsy, and I have almost had a complete recovery at this point. Even though this was a very scary episode, I needed to stick with my imagery and visualize what I wanted instead of what I didn't want.

You too can select the outcome of certain situations using the power of your mind and by learning how to direct energy. There are so many research studies being funded today that are attempting to validate these findings, and personal experience has taught me that everything is energy. I have learned how to determine the frequency of a situation based on feeling and intuition. Fear has a very low frequency, and love and faith have a very high frequency.

If you are in a situation filled with fear and anxiety, you can pull the energy up by adjusting your thoughts deliberately and the energy will follow. EEG is also very effective for helping with this on a neurochemical level.

Using Creative Visualization with Other People

When I was younger, I read all about creative visualization in Shakti Gawain's book of the same name. Discovering how I could create what I saw in my mind was pretty heady material for a 12-year-old, but I was a quick and interested learner! The great part of being exposed to this at such a young age was I realized that I wasn't a victim of life's circumstances. I took this to mean, *Wait a minute . . . I really am in charge here.*

This was so empowering to me, even if I wasn't quite sure how to always incorporate it into my life in those early days. It was the concept that you can do something, and not have life just haphazardly do something *to* you. I loved the idea that if I was having a hard time doing a task, I could see a different path in my mind's eye.

It's even more powerful to visualize as a group if you have the same goal. Some call this a team-building exercise, and I'm the first one to agree that there is power in numbers when it comes to these visualizations. I do this with my *Aware Show* team on our conference calls before we start a new project. We visualize all of the people's lives that will be affected positively as a result of something they heard on our show, thus raising the overall consciousness of the planet. These visualizations set the tone for everything we do.

In addition, it's particularly effective if you visualize together as a family, which is what we do at our house. Jon and I play in this other dimension of pure consciousness that I absolutely know is there, and we've taught our daughter to do the same.

This is a fun, optimistic activity for both adults and children. You can even go around the table and add detail to your visualization based on what the other members of your group are "seeing" in their mind's eye. Together, you can learn to create an aware life on a daily basis.

A Few Final Awarisms:

An aware life means that you will have to practice the following:

* If other people's negative or judgmental energy gets stuck to you, release it and fill yourself up with your own color or energy through a quick visualization. Or as my good friend and healer, Dr. Dain Heer, says, "Return it to from whence it came."

* Know that bad things happen, but your *reaction* to these bad things is what really matters. Of course, you're not immune to negative events, shock, and criticism, but what counts is how you deal with them when they happen.

* Use the visionary technique from this chapter to imagine peaceful, wonderful times in your life and consequently manifest them.

* Celebrate when you reframe a bad situation and get rid of negative energy. That's a victory worth repeating in your mind again and again.

* ※ *

CHAPTER 7

Aware of Your True Potential

I'm sure you'd love to live what I like to call a high-octane life, or up to your true potential. This means living every moment full-out while also building in time to recharge your batteries. At the same time, you realize that other people are going to project their judgments onto you, but you don't allow their projections to stick. Judgments just hold you back, so you eliminate them from your life by realizing that others who weigh you down are not expected to validate you in any way. You realize this, call it out, and move on because you're concentrating on the purpose of why you are doing what you're doing.

I have learned to create on multiple dimensions, or what some call parallel universes. I prefer to call them "parallel levels and realities" because that seems to fit my daily experience of having so many things going on at once. This chapter will explain how to harness and use energy to make what you want to happen a reality, so ultimately you don't have to work so hard. I'm going to take you on this journey where you live with multiple balls in the air and have the energy to juggle them all.

Let's look at my typical day for a minute (although I can't find two days that are exactly the same for me). As a businesswoman, wife, mother, and friend, I *always* have multiple balls in the air, and not dropping even one of them can prove to be the ultimate challenge. As I write this book and run two companies, I'm also going through a move—one of life's ultimate stresses—volunteering at my daughter's school, and creating telesummits for my online business. Of course, everything has a crazy way of needing to happen at exactly the same time.

Some might feel overwhelmed by all of this activity, but I welcome it because I know we all have the power to create on multiple levels. This means that you can manifest everything you want in life—and not just one thing at a time, because life rarely happens just one thing after another. Instead, it's usually a bundle of challenges and opportunities occurring at the same time.

To live full-out and keep the projects afloat, we all need to ask ourselves one simple question: "How capable and creative do I think I am in this moment?" I hope your answer is that you are absolutely capable and astoundingly creative, because that's what will help your life flow no matter what is actually happening in it. It comes down to your belief system.

AWARISM

The first step to creating on parallel levels and realities is to believe that you can. Your belief will guide your multiple successes.

Staying Grateful and Relaxed

Most of us have so much happening at the same time, but we approach our day from a standpoint of negativity. We wake up in the morning and groan, "Oh, I have so much to do today! I don't know how I'm possibly going to get it all done." We feel like there simply aren't enough hours in the day to accomplish our to-do list, and we wonder if we could crawl back under the covers and wish it all away.

A far better way to approach your busy life is to remember that your goal is to be grateful at all times because life is a work in progress. Yes, you have a lot on your plate, but that's a great thing because your life is fluid and exciting with new people, places, and opportunities to explore. You can recognize that there are things you will rush to do in your day, things you don't want to do but have to do, and things that remain a mystery because you're not sure if you're looking forward to them or not.

If you stay in a place of gratitude about all of your categories, you will be able to work on each with an open and clear mind instead of shutting down over one category, and then not being able to work any of the others because you're stuck in a negative vortex.

> ### AWARISM
> Staying in gratitude helps maintain the even flow of your life and will keep you creating with ease. You will not allow yourself to be stopped if any one task isn't working out. You will carry on from a positive place.

I've always got tons of things going at once, which is thrilling to me because I'm like most people who get bored without a lot of activity. Last night, for instance, I was up late working because I didn't have enough time during the day to get all of my research done. My days are usually very full, so several nights a month, after everyone goes to sleep, I go upstairs into my office and do billing and answer e-mails. I just need a little time to juggle those last few balls before I do some meditation to fall asleep after a busy day, happily knowing that I packed a lot of great things into that one 24-hour period.

I like getting work done late at night when the phone isn't ringing and things are quiet. These are my golden hours where I can focus. I sit in my office with our two cats to keep me company, and I have a chance to do research, work on scripts, and dive into the many topics that endlessly fascinate me. I really love what I do, and if there were more hours in a day, I would do more of the same.

Even so, I work hard to keep my life in balance. To that end, I build in downtime with nothing scheduled at least one or two days a week, allowing all sorts of fun to seep in, and intervals to meditate or devote to self-improvement. My days revolve around family and work, in that order, and I have the utmost respect for moms who stay home.

Imagine all the balls *they* have in the air, with children who have different needs and probably attend different schools. Factor in the homework, activities, and occasional illnesses, and those moms are juggling as fast as they can, doing so many things at the same time.

AWARISM

Recognize what relaxes you in the moment. Go through life aware of the joys around you that instantly give you a break, including listening to the laughter of a child, sitting on the cool grass, or smelling the fragrant spring breeze.

You have to recognize joy in the moment—you can't anticipate when it will come up, so make sure to take full advantage of it. When your favorite song comes on the radio as you're pulling into the driveway, for instance, take some time to enjoy it, calm down, and prepare yourself before you walk in the front door.

Check in with Yourself and Recharge

There are times when all of us feel that life is moving too quickly. We're tired and a bit cranky, and then we see a TV commercial for one of those tropical resorts. Suddenly, the idea of a vacation spent under a palm tree sipping drinks with paper umbrellas in them becomes incredibly inviting . . . although we can barely reach for the keyboard to book reservations because we're that tired. Sure, we can do it all, but the question remains, how do we do it all without burning ourselves out?

Even while you're trying to live a high-octane life, it's important to allow yourself recharging moments. The other day, for instance, I had just finished back-to-back radio shows, plus a parent-teacher conference at my daughter's school. Our family was up very late the night before finishing a science project, and then I wrote TV-show scripts until two in the morning. Although I was in gratitude for all the wonderful things happening in my life, I was also bone tired. I was still yawning after a cup of coffee, so I did something you rarely see anyone do anymore.

I pulled my car over in the Starbucks parking lot, which was perfectly safe, and locked the doors before taking a catnap. I went on what my daughter and I call a "noise diet": I turned off the radio, silenced my cell phone, put the seat back, and mentally relaxed every muscle in my body. I imagined a trap door at the base of my lower spine and released all of the energy that might have stuck to me that wasn't mine, letting it flow out of my body. Then I allowed the bright light of divine energy to wash over me, filling me up with energy and protection from pure Source. This practice helps me get rid of anything that isn't in harmony with me and allows me to operate with all of my own energy.

Fifteen minutes later, I woke up refreshed and ready to meet the next six tasks head-on. I was so happy that I had taken a little time for myself, in the solitude I could find, to recharge.

I also learned about "grounding" in one of my meditation classes. You see, sometimes we allow very strong energies to stick to us, which can start to edge out our own essence. You know the feeling when you don't feel like yourself, you're lethargic, and you have a hard time making decisions? This is because you're only operating with half of your own energy. On a daily basis, you need to dump out those other frequencies and fill back up with your own.

An easy way to do this is by choosing a color you are in affinity with (it will usually be the first color that comes to mind). Imagine filling your energy field with that color completely, edging out any other colors that are not aligned with yours. This is a visualization technique that will restore your own energy.

When your day is filled with multitasking and being distracted by technology, negative news, or mind chatter, it's important to check in with yourself to see if you have lost your power or foreign energies have zapped you along the way. The faster-paced our world becomes, the more we need to master this tool of clearing our energy field and refilling with our own vibration. If all of a sudden you feel like you're swimming in molasses, check your grounding. Has it disappeared?

AWARISM
Reground yourself by simply breathing deeply, being mindful, and deepening your awareness. When you establish your connection with the core of the earth and the God of your heart, you'll be able to handle a full day with grace and ease.

Taking off your shoes and walking on the earth is one of the most grounding things you can do. Trust me on this: As I write these words I'm sitting and watching my daughter's soccer practice with my bare feet in the grass, and it feels great!

The Importance of Giving to Others

Giving to others is key to living a high-octane life because it takes the focus off yourself and keeps you from becoming self-absorbed in your daily drama. The minute you give to someone else, it has a sneaky way of recharging your own batteries. The old adage is absolutely true: The more you give, the more you receive. Contributing to the welfare of others refills your own cup in ways you can't imagine. But never give in order to receive—instead, give unconditionally and be grateful for the ability to be of contribution to others.

Dr. Dain Heer, a good friend and an amazing healer, once made a brilliant distinction between being of service versus being of contribution. In one of the many interviews I've done with Dain, he suggested that being of service indicates you are a servant and comes from a place of lack, but being of contribution offers something graciously and unconditionally to someone. This changed the way I say those words forever.

AWARISM
Being of contribution will forever be my choice
when talking about giving to others.

I was physically exhausted after a very long day recently, and I still wanted to go see my parents. A couple of friends who were trying to sell their home needed some help, so before I left, Jon asked, "Could you just talk to them for a few minutes about their house and explain how they can create the outcome that they desire?" I didn't hesitate because our friends were a little stuck—and in return, ten minutes of talking to them reenergized me in a way that I never could have predicted. It was really validating and exciting to be a part of this conversation, while it also felt good physically and emotionally to leave my issues for a moment and focus on someone else. Our conversation helped me stay energized on my long drive to see my mom and dad.

On another occasion, a friend of mine called late to tell me about a problem she was having with her daughter, who kept talking back and acting out in disrespectful ways. I gave this mom the validation she needed, and suddenly all of my overwhelming thoughts about writing radio scripts and setting up meetings for the following day seemed to evaporate. I hung up the phone feeling like I could start another day, and so glad that I could be of some help to my friend.

AWARISM
Helping others quiets your mind and releases your own restless energy. It's a complete win-win situation.

There are people who will say, "How can I help others when I have so much on my own plate?" My mother-in-law often tells me, "You're doing too much. You're overcommitting yourself." She's right in suggesting that it's absolutely necessary to learn the art of saying no, and I am trying to do that. That's tough for a people pleaser like me who wants to help everyone for the sheer joy of doing it. Again, it's about finding a balance between helping others and asking for help, which is something I am gradually learning to do with the support of my very capable teams.

It's All about Team

One of the best ways to live a great life is to work in teams. Personally, I love motivating people who have purpose and passion behind what they do, and then work with them toward a common goal. The radio station I'm on has operated for over 50 years on a 90 percent volunteer basis because of its mission-driven programming. The people who work there are passionately committed to conscious social issues and want a platform to communicate about them. It's a fantastic team that has made this station strong for several decades.

The same is true for my business that provides audiences for TV shows, which I have owned for 20 years. The people who make up these audiences have an opportunity to earn money without having a lot of qualifications, which is a blessing to many in this current economy and especially to students and stay-at-home moms.

My associates run the company like it's their own. They are incredibly dedicated and hardworking, and we all operate like a family, which contributes to the bigger picture of staying together. I've empowered them to make decisions on the fly and trust them to do a great job, which they always do. The same goes for my *Aware Show* team, where everyone is aligned with this beautiful goal of communicating important messages that change so many lives. It's an inspiring mission, and each day on the show, we send out those messages to listeners who in turn are able to heal their own lives.

Thanks to my team on the show, I have a card tacked on my wall that reads, "I'm writing you from my first year at Harvard. I never would have gotten here without listening to your shows." I can only imagine who this Harvard student will touch in her life because of listening to certain messages created by us—not just me, but *us*—on the airwaves. That story helps me live a full-on life, and puts me in a position of eternal gratitude. I can only do all that I do because of my teams, as they help me create possibilities. Together, we support each other to do what we do best and, in turn, the ultimate goal is to help others.

Now, I've seen it work the other way when it comes to forming the wrong team around you. When you surround yourself with individuals who are not aligned with your vision, it just creates disharmony and no one lives their true potential. If someone doesn't tune in to your mental bandwidth and feelings toward what you're creating, then it only serves to create frustration.

How Do You Know If You Have Surrounded Yourself with the Right Team?

A few tips:

* Make a list to help you attract the right person to you. What do you want in this new team member? What qualities would you like them to have? You might write down something like, "I want to attract someone who is in alignment with our mission, who is reliable, capable, punctual, grateful, a self-starter, and an independent thinker."

* Have the vision. You *must* vibrate at the frequency of what you want. In other words, close your eyes and hold the vision of whom you want in your mind. Keep this vibration in your mind through-out the day. The right person will then come along attuned to that vibrational frequency, making for a perfect match.

* Make sure you go through an interview process where you ask several key questions about how the person works and what the job means to them on a personal level. You can immediately tell if someone doesn't really care, or if they're in fact passionate about what you're trying to accomplish. Also, ask them what their goals are in working with the company and see if they're in alignment with what is possible.

* During the interview process, don't just ask about the person's background. Ask them what they would do in certain situations. It's a great way to find out if the person will go beyond the call of duty. Ask them, "Let's say you walked into this situation on the job. What would you do?"

* Ask yourself if that person will be there for you in a pinch. People will get sick or things will break down at work—is this team member going to stick around when the going gets tough? Will they step up when necessary?

* Use your intuition. Even if everyone else is telling you that this person is perfect, allow your intuition to dictate. If something feels wrong, it probably *is* wrong.

Final Awarisms:

* Build teams that will help with your mission, using vibrational-matching techniques while also relying on your personal intuition to tell you who is the right match.

* Realize that others who try to stop you from living a full-on life might have projection issues and are trying to fit you into their model of the world. Don't take on their issues.

* Realize that helping others is your calling, and then reap the benefits of taking yourself out of your own daily drama.

* All human beings need recognition. Take the time to acknowledge those in your world who are doing great things as a way of affirming them.

* * *

CHAPTER 8

Aware and Not Stressed Out

I definitely live a high-octane life, and most of my days are very full. For example, today I started out with an early-morning conference call strategizing for *The Aware Show*'s upcoming events. Then while sitting in traffic, I addressed an issue on the set for my audience company. I hired three new people. I picked up a supplement for healthy hair from one of my favorite Chinese-herb shops on the way to pick up my daughter and a few other kids from school. Then I grabbed a snack and dropped them off at soccer practice, coaching them along the way on how to deal with mean authority figures (their coach is a yeller). And I was still not done.

We've all read countless stories that stress is bad for our health and leads to weight gain, heart disease, and a host of other emotional and physical issues. We're told to reduce our stress, which sounds like a solid idea, but how does one accomplish that in this crazy-busy world?

Personally, I don't let things linger too long or nag at me. The idea is to make each moment and each conversation complete before moving on to the next one so that I don't let things carry over to the end of the day, where stress often compounds.

AWARISM
When it comes to stress, take small steps and deal with things as they come—try not to carry all of it to the end of the day. Instead, resolve as many things as possible, and move on to be fully present in the next moment.

I also handle tension through my communication with God, Spirit, or whoever will listen. I am constantly checking in with the God of my heart to make sure I am aligned with my purpose for that day. I am constantly looking inward and making sure that my conversations and actions are aligned with the highest good. If they're not, I try to catch myself and get back on track.

I have another simple method that keeps me aware of how to deal with the stress in my life: I remember that it is under my control, so I choose to manage my stress instead of allowing it to manage me. You might say, "That sounds like a really good idea in theory, Lisa, but what is the practical approach?" Well, I just keep focused during trying times and remind myself that the most important things in life are love, family, and health. Is this challenging situation a threat to them? If not, I can manage it.

Let's say my computer crashes. Am I annoyed to have potentially lost my work? Of course, but this event doesn't really affect my health or loved ones. So the first step in this management is for me to calmly work toward fixing the problem without allowing it to push my buttons. In other words, I try to make sure that each potentially stressful situation has some type of solution. I like solutions, and this chapter is all about the ones that can help you reduce the amount of stress in your own life.

Gratitude and Action

Whenever you're experiencing stress, one of the most helpful techniques to keep you aware of the big picture is to practice the art of gratitude. Remember what you *do* have. Some people are prone to doomsday thinking, and believe that their life is over because of a financial problem or a job snafu. If this is you, try to live in a state of mind where you spend your days focusing on what you've got: A great partner? A beautiful child? A wonderful pet? Loving friends?

For example, I know a couple whose home burned down. It was so tragic because all of their sentimental items, like precious photo albums and mementos, were gone—along with their clothes, furniture, papers, and so on. Yet when I saw them a few months after the fire, I marveled at how well they were coping with this life-changing event.

As the wife said, "Lisa, I'm safe. My husband, kids, and pets are fine. Instead of getting stressed out daily about what we don't have anymore, I focus on what we *do* have in our lives, which is a lot if you really think about it."

She told me that of course they had gone through shock and grief around the fire, but now they were stronger than ever as a family because they were all "in" when it came to their action plan. Their daily concern was no longer "Woe is us," but "How can we rebuild? How can we reconnect? How can we start over? How can we deal with the insurance company?"

Going into action really does help the stress dissipate. When you're busy and moving forward, there is usually not enough time to allow your mind to get stuck in the loop of, "What am I going to do?"

AWARISM
Try to remove the worry from the situation and focus on the action you can take today. Otherwise you will keep yourself awake all night trying to resolve the situation.

This can be particularly useful when it comes to financial concerns. One of the biggest stresses in the modern world is money, and it's also one of the leading causes of divorce. I've known many couples who have thrown away their relationship instead of trying to resolve their financial issues.

Recently, Jon and I were very stressed out because our house wouldn't sell. We were paying two mortgages, which left us a little freaked out. If you want to have a relationship test, then try to sell a house in a down market with a real estate agent who essentially wants you to dump it. You can't do that because you need that money for your new house, which means the stress is daily because real estate issues take a long time to fix.

Yes, my husband and I were worried, but in an aware relationship like ours we made a new rule. First, we never yelled at each other over the situation or made the other person "wrong." I was the one who wanted us to move and he didn't, so it would have been easy for Jon to point a finger and say, "What did you get us into?" He never did, and instead helped us find a better real estate agent as we worked together to make smart choices to get out of our dilemma. In the end, the stress of navigating complicated financial burdens made our bond even tighter because we came through it together.

I think the most important and aware thing you can do during financial stress is to go into some kind of action plan starting with your mind. Deep down, you will choose not to go to that stressed-out, *I'll-be-homeless,* A-to-Z type of thinking. Instead, you will focus on the fact that you know you have the get-up-and-go, motivation, and inspiration inside of yourself to make it work because you've done so before in your life, and will again.

If you look back at all of the stressful events in your life that you have made it through, sometimes better than you could have imagined, then you can use this memory to help you get through the next set of stressful events. Use it as a reminder that you can work things out as you have in the past. Trust yourself more, and trust the divine—it will help you relax through the process.

AWARISM
In times of financial stress, remind yourself that this is only temporary. Do not get sucked into a negative thought pattern where you convince yourself that you'll dwell in poverty for the rest of your life. Visualize, meditate, pray.

Don't Waste Time Fixating

The other day, a friend of mine told me a story about how a high-school classmate had e-mailed her out of the blue, both to say hello and spend a whole lot of time re-hashing a fight they had 20 years ago, which was still bothering her to this day. My friend couldn't believe that she'd received this rather nasty message on her 50th birthday of all times. She just couldn't let it go—she told me, plus six other friends, about that e-mail over and over again until it gained the momentum of a runaway train.

The birthday girl and I discussed how it was the wrong day for an old friend to send a mean note, and how it was unfair that a fun celebration was interrupted by something so mean-spirited and angry. "It's unfortunate, but you can't fixate on that message, especially on this special day," I said to my friend.

Why is it that we fixate on what's wrong—and not what's right—with our lives? You could have the best day, with your boss lavishing on praise for that amazing sale that will garner new business. Meanwhile, your husband calls to say, "I love you," for no other reason than he really does love you. Your child gets an "A" on that tough history paper that he was sweating for a week. Life is sweet . . . and then some lady cuts you off in traffic and flips you the bird. All of a sudden that little birdie becomes the "head-line news," and the story you repeat to others for days. You're not singing your own praises about a great day at work or on the home front; instead, you're living (again and again) the unfairness of a total stranger who, in a two-second time span, drove into your area and then gave you even more negative energy with a flippant flip of a finger.

Most of us are very good at fixating on what's wrong, which is the exact opposite of living a full-on life. When you fixate, you're the one who is taking the wind out of your own sails, and by repeating moments of fear, failure, or basic unfairness, you're actually living in a state of stress that's unhealthy to mind, body, and soul.

Yes, strange, unfair, and even bad things will happen in a lifetime, and you have to allow yourself to process them. Take the case of the mean e-mail my friend received. In order to live a 500-watt day for her big 5-0, I told her to sort out her emotions by saying, "I feel disappointed that my old friend would send me this sort of e-mail on my birthday. I feel my need for kindness and respect has not been met. I feel misunderstood."

When you start to express your own personal needs, which are often the root of your fixation, only then will you reach the core issues, which are usually unmet needs or hurt feelings. When you're honest with yourself about the root of your fixation and admit that someone hurt you, then you're well on your way when it comes to dissipating the emotions involved with the actual event.

Bill Stierle is a communication expert who uses techniques from Dr. Marshall Rosenberg's Nonviolent Communication, which he has taught to my family and me. "This type of communication style is based on a language of compassion and provides the skills needed to bypass automatic judgment, criticism, blame, or shame," he says. Bill has been a huge help to Jon and me. He was our parent coach and taught us how to raise an empowered child, and he also mediated family conflicts in positive ways that have resulted in a lasting impact.

The other day my daughter came home fixated on the fact that she did not win an art competition at her school. She was quite disappointed because she poured her heart into her painting and said that it was the very best she had ever done on canvas.

Since she felt it was her best, she went into the art competition feeling confident that she would win a prize. When she came home with nothing, there were tears. "It's just not fair, Mommy!" she said.

It was my job as her mother to help her not fixate on her lack of a trophy or certificate while still acknowledging that she was disappointed. "I hear you," I told Kayla. "I know you feel disappointed. I understand."

She said, "But my friend said mine was the best. And how come this technique of visualization you taught me didn't work? I visualized myself winning the art competition."

"Sometimes we can't control everything, and we definitely can't control others," I replied. "With the art competition, there might be criteria you don't know about that went into the judging. And not winning doesn't mean that you're not a great artist, because you are—you don't need a judge to tell you that."

In the end, I didn't try to fix it for her or explain that it wasn't fair or that the teachers didn't know what they were doing when they were judging. I didn't make those sorts of needless excuses for her that would just allow her to continue to fixate. I listened to her and allowed her to get it out, so we could move on as a family.

AWARISM

We're so quick to want to fix things, deny them, or override them instead of facing the core emotions that truly hurt us. Instead of shoving pain down, let's recognize our disappointments by focusing on our unmet needs. That takes the heat off of the stressful moment and stops us from needlessly fixating.

Keep from Getting Sucked into Your Rage

When you're living an aware life, it's important to avoid black holes that tend to pull you down into a churning mess of negative emotions. It's very easy in this hectic world to get sucked into a momentum of negativity until that's all you can focus on.

The other night, for instance, I was dealing with a very exhausting day where each meeting went longer than expected, causing me to get behind in my tasks. This meant that at 10 at night, I had to wander into my office to do the research to write four scripts. I could have fallen down the black hole of, "My life is hard and nobody understands how hard I work, and it's also unfair that I don't get to go to sleep." But honestly, what was the point of hovering above that black hole and allowing the vortex of negativity to pick up momentum until I was swirling and churning in the darkness? On this very late night that didn't end until the wee hours, I instead told myself, "I know this is only temporary. Tomorrow night I will be sleeping next to my husband and getting my rest."

At a soccer game the other day, one of the dads went ballistic when his daughter got unfairly checked and the ref didn't call a foul. Several minutes passed and he was still screaming, refusing to get off of it. Other parents were upset, but they calmed down in minutes. The über-upset dad couldn't stop his brain and continued to yell at the other parents now. It was like his brain was on a drug and he couldn't control the chemicals. I actually looked at him compassionately until he finally walked away and sat on a bench alone.

Luckily, he knew that it was time to walk away, decompress, and take a few deep breaths. He knew his spiral was out of control and took action to get back under control. In the moment of his fit, he was certainly experiencing the addiction of that rush where you make rash decisions and don't act in the most compassionate way possible.

> ### AWARISM
> In stressful situations, weigh the degree of stress.
> There is a major difference between dealing with the stress of death in the family versus money woes or even something so basic as someone cutting you off in traffic. Make sure that you're not overreacting and making every stressful situation equal—because they're not.

Stress, Your Body, and Your Brain

You might have to ask yourself: Are you aware that you're addicted to stress? Perhaps you live in such a stressed-out zone that you're addicted to the rush that it provides and find yourself actually bored when there is nothing to solve or fix. Do you turn daily annoyances —the long line at the supermarket, the guy who cuts you off in traffic—into major freak-outs? Are you calling your friends because some service worker was rude? Are you fuming when that lady races to the counter at the dry cleaners in front of you?

I've found that living at such a high boil is just not worth it, because most little things do not warrant a big response that might compromise your immune system. In fact, when you're about to get stressed out, ask yourself: "Is this worth stressing my immune system over?" Suddenly, that guy who wanted a refund isn't that important.

There have been times in my life when I've been under so much strain that I've needed to pay attention to every single thought. I recently interviewed Dr. Baskaran Pillai, a spiritual teacher who is an enlightened master from the South Indian Siddha tradition. We were talking about stressful thoughts, and he told me that in his meditations, he looks at them as visitors in a hotel. This gave me a great visual of a "thought hotel": If a stressful thought comes to visit, it is a guest, you observe it, and then you watch it leave. It is not welcome to stay long.

According to Dr. Pillai, in the beginning it can take the non-trained mind several hours to clear those types of thoughts. After months of practice, however, this process gets shorter and shorter.

AWARISM
If you can micromanage one thing, it's your own thoughts. Be diligent about keeping them in a forward-moving direction. If a negative thought enters, change the story and move it into a positive pattern.

I know that the minute my thoughts enter the negative zone, I'm allowing a chemical release in my brain that compromises my immune system. Therefore, I limit things in my life that cause negative thought patterns, like that endless complaining session with a girlfriend. Now when negative thoughts come in, I imagine them suppressing my immune system, and immediately put them in my thought hotel.

Remember, your thoughts are hugely important when it comes to stress. And your job is not to harbor that stress, because it only serves to hurt you.

Ways Stress Affects Your Body

* Compromised immunity issues: If you're stressed out, then your body is weaker and often unable to muster up its full ability to fight diseases and infections.

* Dental issues: If you're stressed out, you're much more likely to grind your teeth at night. This leads to temporomandibular joint (TMJ) problems, which can cause face and jaw pain.

* Unhealthy skin: The American Academy of Dermatology in a study has shown that stress worsens skin conditions such as rosacea, psoriasis, and acne. Stress is also dehydrating to your skin, which ages you.

* Memory loss: If you're frazzled and can't find your wallet, there is a medical reason for this. Long-term stress over weeks and months actually disrupts communication between your brain cells while also impeding your brain's ability to store information and create memories.

* Inability to concentrate: Ever try to read when you're stressed? Your brain will rebel. A study showed that medical students studying for exams didn't focus as well when under stress, but during a non-stressful period received high scores from their increased focus.

Dr. Daniel Amen is the founder of the Amen Clinics, which has the world's largest database of functional brain scans relating to behavior; that is, they can actually tell if someone's brain is predisposed to negative thinking. Through these scans, Dr. Amen is able to locate where the brain is misfiring and where that is causing troubled behavior and suffering.

I have found one of the best ways to retrain the brain is through brain-wave entrainment technology. This is usually recorded neural-auditory programming using sub-audible beats that can normalize brain-wave patterns for deeper sleep or better focus, to relieve stress, or for forward-pacing motivation. Since some of the latest research shows that 90 percent or more of our behavior stems from the unconscious mind, I think it is the best idea to use these technologies that target the unconscious mind to create lasting effects. Some of my favorites are done by John Assaraf, Brent Phillips, and the Institute of HeartMath.

This technology can be listened to on headphones, and it usually layers in subliminal affirmations with binaural beats, allowing the brain to enter into a *theta* state. In this relaxed state, the brain begins to resolve issues and reorganize, and depending on the type of technology you listen to, can even help you feel blissful and calm. This is brain-nastics, for sure!

Take Breaks and Laugh!

A friend of mine just lost her mom after nursing her through a long illness. It followed that the stress level in the house was on high alert—or had become the chronic strain of a caregiver situation, which many baby boomers are facing these days. Once her mom passed, my friend went through a grieving period, which was naturally difficult, too. After so much stress in her life, I asked how she was coping, and her answer was simple: "It's all about the little moments." Eureka! Even in a tough situation, there are those little moments when you can step out of it and find joy. You just have to be aware enough to *find* these moments and not let them pass you by.

Why not try to bring even a small amount of laughter into your life—especially if you haven't laughed in a long time? I can promise you that it feels so good. In fact, laughter prompts your brain to release "feel-good" neurotransmitters: dopamine, serotonin, and an array of endorphins. In the process, you also stimulate circulation and increase your intake of oxygen.

When I'm in a highly tense time in life, I love to watch a silly movie with outrageous humor. No, I'm probably not going to see the best movie of the year when I watch *The Pink Panther* with Steve Martin (a classic for our family), but I doubt I'll see one that makes me laugh harder. Or I'll run around the backyard with my daughter, who I know will do something to make me giggle. In the end, it's about allowing myself some bliss because I deserve it and so does my body.

AWARISM

Our bodies are not meant to live in a stress zone, and sometimes the kindest thing you can do for your physical body is to put yourself in situations where you will smile.

I used to get four or five hours of sleep a night until that caught up with me. I also was never much of a napper, but I've become a big fan. I've found that even ten minutes in the car or on the couch with my eyes closed can recharge my entire day and reorganize my brain. Try it sometime and you will understand what I'm talking about.

It's good to take those breaks to just clear your mind and renew your energy. And when you do close your eyes, it's much easier for your mind to go into a mode of resolving the issues that have come up that are gnawing at you. Sleep is a very important way to relieve stress, as you work a lot out when you're slumbering—think of it as a long meditation.

In addition, the National Sleep Foundation has found in studies that a short nap of 20 to 30 minutes can increase your short-term awareness and provide you with improved alertness and performance without leaving you groggy or interfering with your nighttime sleep. In fact, a short nap can extend alertness for a few hours. A study at NASA on sleepy pilots and astronauts found that a power nap improved their performance by 34 percent and their alertness by 100 percent.

Look at your nap like a pleasant break or even a mini-vacation where you can rejuvenate. Famous nappers include Albert Einstein, Winston Churchill, John F. Kennedy, Thomas Edison, and Ronald Reagan, all of whom admitted that they enjoyed some afternoon rest periods.

In addition, there are many helpful books and programs that offer stress-relief techniques. I find that music and being out in nature help me to release tension, as does laughter and practicing the art of gratitude. In my most stressed-out times, I will actually say out loud five things that I'm grateful for in that moment. If that's not enough, I'll put on my headphones and listen to beautiful music that takes me to another place. Prayer is also a great way to get rid of stress. Many people practice breathing exercises to decompress. It's important to find what stress relief works for you and to move on from what doesn't work.

Finally, a great way to reduce stress is to practice compassion, which is something the Dalai Lama talks about in depth. His Holiness believes that compassion can solve most of the world's problems. You just need to be aware of the moment and substitute compassion for anger.

FINAL AWARISMS:

* Have a "let it go" chalkboard (or eraser board) and write down all the negative things that happen. Then read them aloud before erasing them. The latest neuroscience research conducted by Professor Mark Waldman says that putting those negative things out in the open desensitizes you to those particular issues and then causes you to be done with them.

* Find what it takes for you personally to let go of your stress and incorporate that into your daily routine. I like to take naps, go out in nature, or be in a deep state of gratitude.

* Realize that life will present challenges. Look for core-issue feelings in order to acknowledge what is really bothering you.

* If you dwell or fixate, then that will take up all of your energy and bandwidth. It's fine to say to yourself, "This stinks. This hurts." Recognize the unfairness, hurt, and unkindness, and then realize that your need for consideration wasn't met. Don't ignore it, stuff it down, or put it away for another day. Release it.

* * *

CHAPTER 9

Aware of Life's Roadblocks

When things go wrong for me, they tend to go wrong in a big way. Take what happened recently when I planned to go to Denver for a major meeting concerning the radio show. I made reservations several weeks prior for both my producer and me to go out of town, and then glanced at the paperwork a few days before the trip. I was thrilled that I'd gotten such a low rate for a round-trip ticket. When I looked again, though, I realized that I had flipped the cities—instead of flying from my home in Los Angeles to Denver, I had both of us flying out of Denver and *into* L.A.

When I called the airline to discuss this annoying mistake, the lady on the phone was perfectly understanding and said this happened all the time, but she absolutely couldn't flip the cities in the right way at that same fare. In fact, thanks to the last-minute nature of having to do a fix-it job here, it was going to cost thousands of dollars to make it right.

The same day of this airline snafu, someone from my company that fills studio audiences called me with words no one ever wants to hear: "We have a problem." It seemed that an audience member on one of the shows had an epileptic seizure on the set and was being rushed to the hospital, which delayed the taping of the show. My associate said that he'd keep me posted.

Wait, I'm not done! Earlier that day, I decided to have a little R & R time with my daughter, and she begged me to stop at one of those bouncy trampoline places. As we were bouncing together and really letting loose, Kayla did a cartwheel without looking where she was landing, which was my head. She didn't mean to do it, but she hit me so hard that I saw stars and a major chunk of my hair was ripped out. Not only did it really hurt, but I was mortified because I had all these meetings coming up. After tears and apologies and even more assurances that it wasn't her fault, I drove her to soccer practice with a throbbing headache . . . only to figure out at the last minute that I had the wrong day.

What could I do but laugh? You must at least smile when life, or your child, hits you on the head.

Learn to Reframe the Shocks

What happens when life throws you a major curveball: illness, divorce, or job loss; or a host of other disappointments, ranging from a fender bender to that water pipe that just collapsed most of the kitchen ceiling? How can you live in a state of flow and guide yourself successfully through disappointments?

It's time to learn how to "reframe the shocks" to move on and get your life back. Bad things are going to happen —in fact, life itself is a constant series of challenges both small and large. It's all about learning how to deal with your roadblocks in order to move past them. In the case of my airline reservations, I didn't accept that I needed to pay thousands of dollars to fix the problem. In fact, I kept calling and calling, explaining the situation each time, until I found a very nice woman at the airline who waived the change fee.

Jon and I also decided that while I was in Denver, he would go to Palm Springs with our daughter and stay with some friends. It seemed like a great time for a little father-daughter bonding while I was away. We reframed the shock of the airline incident by "dancing" long enough to find a good solution and then making a few new moves that would keep everyone happy.

AWARISM
Dealing with your life's troubles should be thought of as a dance. There usually isn't just one move, but many moves that will create the choreography of reframing the shock in a way that will help you find success.

The first step in dealing with life's roadblocks is to realize that aggravating things will happen, but the toll that they take on your well-being, your mental and physical health, and the overall state of your life is entirely up to you. For example, when I discovered that Kayla's soccer practice was on another day, I took the opportunity to celebrate this gift of some unexpected alone time with her. I didn't berate myself for making a mistake, but instead rolled down the windows of the car, opened the sunroof, turned the dial to some great tunes, tilted the seats back, and took a half-hour bonding break with my daughter. We truly made lemonade out of lemons by accepting our fate and making an even better plan for our time together.

The alternative would have been to dwell on that nagging feeling of aggravation or even rage, moaning about how it wasn't fair that we drove out of our way when there wasn't even practice. We reframed the shock by immediately thinking of this free time as a gift to enjoy. Suddenly, there was no room to be sad or mad because we were having one of those spontaneous mother-daughter adventures.

AWARISM
Live for the little moments that pull you out of the darkness and give you a true and better perspective.

Now, let's return to the very bad day that I experienced, and I'll explain how I reframed those shocks in order to not reach for a box of Kleenex while crawling back under the covers! When my co-worker told me that there was a problem on the set, I took a moment to make sure the audience member was in the right hands, then went into action to make sure the rest of the people were taken care of in the right way.

In the case of my airline mistake, I was mad at myself and allowed myself to experience that anger. Several moments later, I added the extra anger that is almost a given when dealing with a bureaucracy like a major airline. As each "no" piled up on the phone lines while I tried to inexpensively right the wrong, I worked at keeping calm.

I reminded myself that companies like airlines and hotels love to change the rules or make them up as they go along, and I convinced myself that if I just kept calling back, I'd find the right vibrational match in one of the workers who would help me. Sure enough, I finally heard a note of true compassion in a stranger's voice that was bolstered when I admitted that the mistake was my own.

AWARISM

In times of trouble, it is always helpful to admit that you are the one who made the mistake (if it's the truth). You will gain respect from others and even help from them if you own up to your own part in the problem. You must stand up.

Finally, I had to examine the outcome of my daughter kicking me in the head. It was really hard for me not to get upset when it first happened, but I was proud that I didn't because it was an accident and she already felt so bad. Kayla was beating herself up about it, and her mother getting mad wouldn't have helped.

As far as my hair goes, I had to wear it up for a while. At least it wasn't worse than a bump and a loss of hair—God knows I am no stranger to head trauma, and it wasn't that bad. Count your blessings!

Dealing with Guilt and Worry

Guilt and worry are two powerful and destructive forces in many of our modern lives, and they derail our progress when it comes to living an aware life. I'll start with guilt because it's very prevalent for women, who seem to have this invisible force that tugs at them and makes them honestly believe that they're never doing enough. Or perhaps they feel that they're always doing the wrong thing, equaling a heaping pile of guilt that acts as a fog in their lives. I'm not immune from it either, especially as someone who is constantly striving to strike a balance between work and my husband and daughter, as well as taking care of my own parents.

Remember the trip to Palm Springs that Jon and Kayla took while I was in Denver? Even though I knew in my heart that they were having the best time, I still felt that wash of guilt come over me because I couldn't be there to make it more of a family vacation. The three of us love to spend time together and it is hard for us to be apart, although it's a necessary part of my work life. I thought it would be fun for Kayla to go on a trip with her dad instead of staying home and calling me to say, "Mom, when are you coming home?" So why did I feel guilty when honestly it was Mom who needed a break? The great news is that I ended up packing a lot into my Denver trip and then had extra time for my daughter at home.

It always amazes me how many things women can juggle (although I know men do this all the time, too). I used to travel from Los Angeles to Denver every single Wednesday to tape a show for Gaiam TV. I'd leave my home at 4 A.M., tape two shows, and then fly back, which had me walking through my front door at 10 P.M. It didn't matter that this was a grueling schedule; the key thing was that I minimized being away from Kayla while she was young, to only one day a week.

Soon I got into the rhythm of this schedule and it became old hat, but I do have to admit now that this type of hit-and-run travel took a toll on my health—and that was something I tried to sweep aside, because minimizing my travel helped me deal with the guilt of being away from home. Finally, I had to check in with myself and admit, "I just can't do this anymore." All of that travel was exhausting, so I looked for alternatives, including moving the show to Los Angeles. You never know unless you ask, and this ended up working. We found a studio to tape all the Gaiam TV shows in L.A., and it worked out better for all involved.

One of the best ways to beat guilt is to look for alternatives; another way is to ease off the controls a little bit. When I feel like I have to do it all, I check in with myself for a quick reminder that my *Aware Show* team can handle anything. When I was involved in a car accident last year and was forced to take some time off, my team kicked in, and everything worked out just fine. As I wrote in a previous chapter, I'm such a huge proponent of teams because most of us juggle so much that we can't and shouldn't do everything solo.

When a woman hit the gas instead of the brakes in the Starbucks drive-through line not long ago, crashing into me at 20 miles per hour while I was at a standstill, I smacked my head hard. (It did make me wonder, *What is the deal with this head of mine? Maybe I should walk around wearing a helmet or not go to Starbucks so often!*) Thank God my daughter wasn't hurt, but my head hit the side of the window, which caused a huge egg to form on the side of my head. Kayla was the rock star in this case—she rushed into the Starbucks and asked for a cup of ice and put it on my head. I was shocked and confused because everything had happened so suddenly. But later I felt guilty that I couldn't take better care of my daughter right after the accident. After we went to the doctor, I found out she was fine.

Guilt plus worry is the modern way of life for many, but I have to confess that I probably don't worry enough. Perhaps that's thanks to the teachings I'm sharing with you in this book! I do know friends, family members, and co-workers who worry so much that it leaves little time or mental bandwidth for the other things in life. Worry is living your life in fear, which is frankly the wrong way to live.

I know families who base their major decisions on their worries, handing down "the worry gene" to the next generation. I call this "anxiety-based parenting" because Mom and Dad are so worried about everything that their child also becomes someone filled with anxiety. The solution to this is present-time thinking.

I'd like to share a story with you of what this type of thinking can accomplish—it's an example of what is possible, even in the most extreme situations. Recently, my husband and I were on vacation in Bali with a couple of our dear friends, having the best time ever. The four of us found ourselves on a beach that served dinner on the sand at sunset, with a backdrop of the beautiful colors of the setting sun and the sound of the waves crashing in front of us. The husbands decided to jump in the water and do a little bodysurfing until dinner. Then the unthinkable happened: A huge wave came crashing down on our friend, driving him headfirst into the ocean floor and knocking him unconscious. Jon, an ex-lifeguard, pulled him out of the water to shore.

What happened next was the most extraordinary exercise of present-time thinking imaginable. It turns out that our friend had broken five vertebrae in his neck, and underwent emergency surgery within five hours of the accident. The surgery was a success, fusing together the five separated vertebrae . . . and this couple's weeklong vacation turned into a life-changing journey into the unknown. They had to stay in Bali in the intensive care unit at the local hospital while he recovered, because he was unable to fly home in his condition, and it was unclear how long the healing would take.

Our friends' only option was to live moment to moment and deal with what life had to offer in every given second. The minute they started to think of what could have happened in the past or what might happen in their future, they froze. Instead, while asking the right questions all along, they started their new journey together of healing and living in gratitude for every blessing along the way. Their lives changed forever in a split second on that beach, and they have made the best of it. I am so proud of my friends for their strength and courage to live in present time and for their gratitude for life, as precious as it is.

AWARISM

Worry is a needless emotion and can mostly be categorized as "what if" thinking or spending too much time in the future rather than present time. Most of the time the "what if" never happens, but those who worry are so focused on it that they can actually manifest it. You need to be conscious of your worries and stay in present time as much as possible. Always be cautious, but try to think of worry as a habit that you *need* to break.

For most of us, it's just a bad habit to focus on "what if" scenarios as a way to prepare ourselves for anything that could (and probably won't) happen. Yes, it's good to be prepared, but do be mindful of how much time you are spending on this. If it's over 10 percent, then focus on "what *is*" rather than "what if."

I was raised with worst-case-scenario thinking and somehow knew in my early life that I had to un-train myself from this type of thinking. I have come to know that when you dwell on the worst happening at any moment, you often attract those situations to you and they become a vibrational match. The secondary gain of being a worst-case-scenario thinker is that you get to be right, but this is a nonexistent victory. Who wants to be right and then wade through the most difficult times?

Living your life this way is a dangerous loop because you're always in deep drama, either thinking about disaster or fixing what has gone wrong thanks to your mindset. If disaster happens, deal with the moments in present time, and it will make the journey an experience you will be able to learn from later.

Tips for Dealing with Worry

* Visualize what will go right instead of what will go wrong.

* Don't repeat or dwell on stories of past mistakes. Move on as fast as possible.

* Ask yourself, "What did I learn?" rather than beating yourself up for making a mistake.

* Try to avoid beginning a conversation with the words, "I had the worst day yesterday." Avoid

bringing the negative energy from yesterday into today. Today is a new day.

* Remember that habits like worry become neural patterns.

* Focus your mind on the positive, like that beautiful oak tree and those leaves blowing in that refreshing breeze, rather than focusing on what bad thing could happen. Stay in the present moment.

* Even if you've had a stressful day, commit yourself to having a great night and restful sleep, knowing that tomorrow will be a better day.

There are many people who rely on anxiety-related medications these days, and that subject is between doctor and patient. One of my best ways to relieve worry is not found in a pill bottle, though—it involves sitting, holding my legs with my hands, and chanting. I know this might sound crazy to some people, but I dare them to try it the next time they're in a bad spot. Chanting is actually quite liberating as it's like walking through mazelike places that require your intense concentration, thus deflecting your worry.

I have religious friends who will get out their rosary beads during times of worry, which studies show can significantly decrease cortisol levels. In fact, all of the activities mentioned here work toward decreasing cortisol levels because in their own way, they create a meditative state in the brain.

> ## AWARISM
> Nurturing a pet is another way to decrease your worry levels. While petting a pet or focusing on their care, you tap into a natural human frequency of calm energy. Care for a pet and they will care for you because animals feel that vibration of love very easily.

As I mentioned earlier in the book, it was hard for me to grow up surrounded by so much uncertainty and negativity. When I became an adult, I went through several forgiveness processes, and my sensitive perspectives as a child have now been reframed. I love working with my spiritual teacher, Michael Tamura, where we have gone back into my past through visualization to see what was going on from a neutral perspective, including the karmic perspective of healing my family.

In addition, I've learned so many helpful techniques from the guests I've interviewed over the past 15 years. For example, Dr. Jerry Jampolsky and Immaculée Ilibagiza have both written about their stories of forgiveness and are wonderful experts on the subject. I'm also a great fan of Caroline Myss's "Sacred Contracts" and Debbie Ford's "Shadow Process," and Christopher Howard has helped me become certified in neuro-linguistic programming (NLP) methods.

I have always been the type of person who loves to discover why I do the things I do and why other people do the things *they* do. I suppose this type of curiosity fuels my work, which is why it isn't really work for me at all.

A Space for Healing

Ryan, a man in his 40s, called the radio show the other day to talk about his plight in life as a Realtor working in a post-recession market. He had a concept to start a new business outside of real estate, but didn't really have the finances to begin. Combined with his worries about many new ventures tanking in the first year (or so he'd heard on TV), he was living in a state of extreme worry about his future and his current situation as a Realtor. "I feel paralyzed," he said. "My fears are limiting everything in my life. I can't even take a step forward and go out to meet the people who might finance my new business because I'm too afraid that I would actually get the money and then fail."

It was obvious to both my guest expert and me that day that Ryan was like many other listeners in that he felt betrayed by life and had both worry and trust issues. "Where else are these issues showing up in your life?" I asked him, and his answer was dead silence for what seemed like a long time.

"Are you there?" I gently asked, but knew the answer when I heard a soft sobbing in the background. This man couldn't speak at the moment, and instead found himself weeping on live radio. On most shows, the host would cut to another caller because this is called "dead air," which is a big negative because other listeners could just change stations in that time. But I did something rather new— I allowed the silence, and let the moment naturally unfold.

Basically, I sat with Ryan like you would sit with a friend. I listened to him cry, and then finally said, "I know many emotions are coming to the surface for you. I understand that there might even be issues you don't remember or don't want to speak about today." He continued to sob, and the guest expert began to talk about the concept of past hurts leading to current trust issues. All of a sudden, the phone lines were going berserk with people calling in wanting to help.

I'll never forget the man who called in to say, "Hi, Ryan. I'm a Zen Buddhist. I want to tell you that we are one." Another person called in to tell Ryan that he wanted to help him fund his new venture because the caller only wanted to do business with people who were authentic.

This remains one of my favorite shows ever because, as a group, we tried to allow Ryan to release his pain and feel at one with others to shed his worries. The rest of the group was here for only one reason: emotional support. These types of matches happen frequently on my shows because I allow the space for connection and healing to happen. The blueprint energy of my shows is set in the tone of pure communication and endless possibilities.

Another example came from Sherry, a listener who hated her desk job and had a passion for helping women with body-image issues. In her past, she had been abused and spent most of her free time healing that trauma while taking night-school classes for psychology. She clearly had done a lot of personal development around her issues and wanted to carry on her mission to help others do the same. Then another person called in who was a plastic surgeon. This doctor wanted to get in touch with Sherry to have her work in her office to counsel women before their surgeries to make sure they were doing it for the right reasons.

Time and time again, this type of magic happens, and I am honored to be a part of it.

> ### AWARISM
> One of my favorite techniques I love to do when I am
> upset or worried about something is to realize only a part
> of me is worried and to have a dialogue with that part of me.
> Sometimes, just allowing that part of myself to express my
> worry or fear defuses it. I also realize that the rest of my being
> is okay and perfectly safe in that moment. Eventually the
> worried part of me subsides, and the balanced part of me
> takes over and allows calmness to return.

Find the Lesson in Life's Challenges

I've had so many callers on *The Aware Show* who are in deep emotional pain from different sources. It humbles me to know that they are turning to my radio show to reach out for help. The thing that often strikes me is that most people do not reframe events that are less than pleasurable in life. The best advice I've ever heard is what I will tell you right now: *When something in your life goes wrong, look for the lesson that you can learn from this event. Somewhere there is energy that is trying to teach you something.*

For example, I had a caller who was part of sweeping layoffs at his corporation. In his 50s, he was beside himself because his savings had dwindled and he was experiencing that gripping, heart-pounding, breath-stealing fear that wakes you up in the middle of the night.

About a year later, he called back to say, "Lisa, my layoff was absolutely one of the greatest blessings of my life. Each day, my boss and co-workers were emotionally abusing me. At my age, I just tried to make it through the ten-hour days without making any waves. Did I also mention that I was overworked to the point of exhaustion, which was starting to take a toll on my health?"

When this man got the boot from his company, it forced him to look for a different job—and he found a great one, with a wonderful boss and supportive peers. "Getting fired was the first step when it came to finding my dream job," he told me in a happy voice, noting, "I sleep like a baby now." What was the lesson in his firing? He reframed the situation in his mind to state now that being fired was the best thing possible, and the lesson was that good jobs with nice people were out there if you look hard enough. His other lesson was that no one should have to suffer through abuse silently.

AWARISM
Quite often our biggest life failures push us into our greatest successes. Always put life on pause and look for the lesson in each disappointment.

The definition of *perturbation* is "a deviation of a system or process from its regular or normal state or path caused by an outside influence." It's the old tale of sand abrasively rubbing within the oyster to create the shiny pearl; that type of agitation is needed for the gem to arise. This is often the case when it comes to our personal growth—we get so tired of doing something the difficult way that the frustration we experience causes us to act in a different and easier way. This kind of perturbation, or deviation, is often spawned by the pure frustration of systems breaking down.

A woman I know was involved in an intense class-action lawsuit against a life-insurance company. She was representing millions of people and went up against 12 attorneys backed by a billion-dollar insurance company. She didn't win her suit, but guess what? The fact that she lost launched this rocket of desire within her to go on a personal journey where she taught others about how to read a life-insurance policy's fine print. All of a sudden, this woman found her passion throughout a challenging time that actually cost her a great portion of her life's savings.

At moments like this, you can look at the situation in two ways: You can become completely disabled by it and never get out of bed. Or you can use it to jump-start what you truly want in life, fueled by the fact that you won't lose again. After experiencing a loss, it's easy to figure out what you want next time.

AWARISM
Intention plus the intensity of emotion equals success. Use your intensity to make possible what others see as impossible. Affirmations only work if you add emotional intensity to them. Sometimes intensity comes from an unexpected event such as a job loss or move. Don't bemoan your fate; instead, stay in your center and use the intensity around current events to move your intentions.

Try Meditation

Since it's a given that everyone will hit a roadblock in life, it's important to find ways to soothe yourself when you are in crisis mode.

My go-to first call is to realize that a challenging time is only temporary, and all I need to do is deal with what's happening in the moment. I found a great soother while doing a show on stress relief where my guest was a meditation expert. I've spoken to many meditation teachers over the years, but there was something special about Dr. Andrew Newberg, because he told me that he'd been doing research on the subject for over 20 years.

I thought, *If anyone is qualified to give advice in this area, it's this man.* Dr. Newberg then said the magic words to me on the air: "Meditation doesn't have to be complicated, or all about sitting in a pose and saying, 'Om.' It can actually be quite simple."

This expert reminded my audience and me that the practice of meditation could take place anywhere, at any time, and it didn't even need to involve sitting—this ancient art form was a highly personal one. "It will be different for everyone. Certain meditations work for certain people and not others," he said. You can even do it in line at the bank simply by standing in gratitude. This isn't the traditional practice of meditation; I call it "practical meditation" or, better yet, "meditation for busy people."

I knew that I had to make meditation a permanent part of my life, although in the past it had been very challenging for me. After the show I did with Dr. Newberg, it became clear that I didn't have to go to an ashram or sit on a mountaintop. When I thought about it, I knew that my meditation would involve walking.

I need to move my body, which means that it can be almost impossible for me to sit still and meditate. Instead of thinking calming thoughts, I tend to fidget and my mind announces, *It's sort of uncomfortable sitting here because my back hurts.* If I really want to clear my head, I prefer to walk around somewhere, as the repetitive movement helps me achieve a state of calm. If I get out and move in nature, it's the best-case scenario for me.

The other great bit of knowledge I received on my show was that you don't have to meditate for an hour—even five minutes will do if that's all the time allotted in your day. Of course, it's great to be able to enjoy a longer session when it comes to this calming activity, but you don't have to rule out meditation altogether if you're super busy.

In addition, I've learned that nothing duplicates the results of meditation. It's a medical fact that there is nothing you can take in pill form, including supplements, which will rid your body of the stress hormone cortisol that has built up during the day. Yet a five-minute meditation will do the job, keeping cortisol from building up in your system.

> ### AWARISM
> If we take little moments to "release our steam," our life will be so much easier and even more energized and thus more productive. If you're experiencing low energy, try meditation as a way to recharge yourself.

A few nights ago, I was answering e-mails before I headed to bed, but then stopped about 20 minutes before I went to sleep. Alone in my office, I found a guided meditation on my computer and turned it on low, so I could hear the music in the background. I sat in a comfortable chair, closed my eyes, and felt my body calming down as my shoulders actually dropped. Taking these 20 minutes to meditate enabled my busy mind to relax and stop working. That way my mind didn't keep going all night, and I could actually enjoy a deeper sleep.

People call my show all the time with the health complaint of insomnia. A nighttime meditation before you go to bed is a very effective way to get to sleep and *stay* asleep.

AWARISM

Build short meditations into your daily schedule.
Even if you're working late, allow yourself those extra
10 to 20 minutes before you go to bed to meditate.
It will both relax you and help you sleep.

Check Back In

It's a fascinating question for most of us: How much of our lives comes down to free will and choice, and how many facets are actually guided by Spirit? I'm not an angel communicator, but I certainly trust in spiritual guidance— as I remain committed to being open to that protection in life in a very practical way. Call it intuition or spirit guides, but I do believe that you must listen for that voice that always comes through to help you navigate your life. All of us know that voice, and quite often it comes through as thoughts that might seem like they are not our own.

Author Sonia Choquette once said to me in an interview that "living life without listening to your intuition is like walking around in the dark all day." It's true, in a sea of mental chatter, intuition will cut through all the muck and give you great clarity when you're deciding what to do in any given situation. All of a sudden, the world seems to stop, and a new thought will come through to you.

Notice that your intuition is always forward thinking. Your job is to listen for this guidance while remaining in the flow of your life, and then use that wisdom to raise your own vibration.

Listeners often want to know if we can actually *ask* for our intuition or spiritual guidance to come into play and help with decision making or wading through murky waters. I do believe that this is entirely possible, and even quite easy to accomplish, especially when our back is up against the wall.

When I was facing certain life questions recently, I went outside, sat down in a quiet spot, and allowed a warm breeze to wash over me. I tried to quiet my mind and listen as my eyes drifted upward to what was almost a full moon. On that cloudless summer night, a scattering of bright stars was my only light. As I swept away the daily issues, I allowed my mind to focus on the life questions at hand, and let my intuition guide me.

I call this exercise my "Check Back In" moment. I was busy living my life, but I knew that I needed to stop, get quiet, and check in with myself to solve a problem. It doesn't cost a dime to schedule these Check Back In moments with yourself, and I advise you to do so often, especially when going through a troubling time.

Think of the Check Back In as your own personal GPS—instead of a satellite or computer, it's your intuition or spirit guides that will get you from point A to B. If you choose to think of this as checking in with your angels, then so be it. That's what I do. I am constantly guided, or else I couldn't life a truly aware life. My dear friend Doreen Virtue has been a guiding light in my life, reminding me that if I listen to the guidance of my angels, I will always be on the right path. I am so grateful for her constant reminders.

AWARISM

When dealing with a major life issue (or even a minor one), it's important to get quiet, sweep away the daily chatter, and check in with yourself. The answers are there. You just have to find the time and the quiet to listen. Do not doubt what you hear, as it is usually the truth. Sometimes sleeping on a big decision can also help you process and get clarity the next day.

One quick note on checking in with yourself: You absolutely do not have to wait for a major life event to do this exercise. Your average day will present you with several challenges where your intuition might be your only guide. Should you allow your daughter to go to that kid's house? Will you listen to the advice of a friend? Is it a good idea to go into business with that person? You can easily get quiet for a minute or two, check in, and find the answers. Once the answer is given, then trust it instead of second-guessing what you've heard.

The other day, I was taking a mountain-bike ride with Jon. The sun was shining and we were having a wonderful time, but then we found ourselves at a crossroads. Should we stay on one path that seemed safe with a bit less spectacular scenery, or should we veer off into the bushes and ride along the side of the cliff? Even while pedaling my bike, I did a quick Check Back In, and my intuition was screaming at me to turn around and not continue on. Of course I listened.

Later, I heard that the cliff ride was full of thorns and the "safe" path had been overgrown. Turning around was the right choice, and I didn't second-guess it. It would have been just as easy to blow right through those thoughts and continue on, but instead Jon and I chose another way that was absolutely right.

Be Conscious of Positive Words

Everything that comes out of your mouth should be positive, so be sure to focus on something you want to bring into your world. You shouldn't say something you don't want, such as, "I hope I'm not one of the 10 people out of 100 that they lay off today," or "I'll be stuck in this little cubicle for the rest of my life." This is an easy way to live if you're aware: If you don't want it, then don't say it. Your words are strongly connected to your destiny.

Speaking in terms of negativity is a bad habit that needs to be broken, like smoking. As adults, we can consciously treat what we don't want like weeds and pluck them from our language. Instead of telling your friend, "I just know that Timmy is going to be that one kid they hold back," it's crucial to focus on the positive and say, "Timmy is trying really hard in school, and I'm so encouraged by his newfound love of reading." Instead of drowning in all the negative thoughts and words, you have spoken the truth, but you have also placed positive energy around your life and events. This is especially important if you're speaking in front of that child.

One example that stands out in my mind was when my daughter and I were at a sushi bar, and a woman sat beside us with her son who was about nine years old. The mother proceeded to tell the waiter how this was the only place they could eat because her son was allergic to wheat, and the rest of the family was eating at another restaurant down the street. I watched as the boy's shoulders dropped and he sank down in his chair. Unknowingly, the mom was making her son feel wrong for having a food allergy, blaming him for something that wasn't his fault.

Instead of saying that something is "hard," reframe it by saying it is something you're working on overcoming. Why do we say what we don't want in life? I've learned that most negative mental programming is in fact self-hypnosis. You immediately leap to the worst-case outcome because you've almost hypnotized yourself to go there. It's the same thing when you sit down at the kitchen table late at night when no one is looking and eat half a chocolate cake. You're sitting there shoveling it in because you're in a total state of hypnosis and just repeating a bad pattern.

How to Stop Negative Thoughts and Self-Talk

If you find yourself in a tailspin where you're verbalizing negative thoughts, try to change the energy by doing the following:

* Take a walk in nature.

* Talk about happy times with a loved one.

* Look at something visually stimulating, like inspiring art.

* Listen to peaceful music. Incidentally, it only takes 20 minutes or less of meditative music to get you into a more blissful, peaceful state. Music also calms the rhythms of the heart.

* Try Holosync, a technology created by Bill Harris. Holosync has been available for 25 years and revolves around listening with

headphones to get your brain into a twilight state before sleep, as it brings you into a deeply relaxed, coherent state. This also increases your tolerance of pain. It's just one of many great sound technology healings that anyone can explore.

* Try Chinese healing music, which is not only beautiful, but there are certain tones to those strings that induce a meditative state as well. Download the music onto your phone so that it's readily available when you need to detox from negative speak or thoughts.

When we repeat negative patterns, we're often in a state of self-hypnosis where we're just continuing those patterns instead of being conscious of what we truly want. Experts believe that 90 percent of what we do is this type of unconscious thinking. To correct it, all you need to do is turn it around and get conscious about your actions. Really, you're going to eat half a cake? Put the fork down and stop. For five minutes, consciously be aware of what you're doing. I'm sure you will walk away from the bad habit, which is the first step in breaking it.

I can't stress enough how you must be ultraconscious of your language, because if you have a negative mind-set, it will come out in your words and then manifest in your life. I've had listeners say that this is a hard thing for them to do because they're so used to going toward the more negative side of life. I remember a woman who called and told me that she needed to get a new home in a better part of town but "could never afford to move." We talked about how limiting beliefs will turn into your realities.

I want to stress that language won't solve all of your problems, and I'm certainly not talking about pie-in-the-sky thinking or being in denial of your issues. However, the right language will start you on your journey of awareness, and help to set you in the right direction so you can think of real solutions. This change in your belief system is a major step if you want to get past life's roadblocks and truly change your circumstances.

FINAL AWARISMS:

* Reframe the shock when something dramatic happens in your life.

* Be aware of when you are caught in a cycle of repeating bad patterns, as this will help you break them.

* Make use of mindfulness and meditation to release your daily tension.

* ※ *

CHAPTER 10

Aware When Experiencing Death and Loss

I once interviewed a Native American elder whose beloved wife had died the year before. It was a tragic loss for this man and his family, and he choose to honor his wife and what she meant to him on the deepest of personal levels. He decided to make an important physical change to mark the passage—he actually cut his long hair as part of the grieving process. Every month, he also did a ritual that reminded him of his lost love, ranging from a special candle ceremony to prayers dedicated to her life. This was especially beautiful to me because he remained aware of her life and their love at a special time that he has marked every month. He spent time with himself and didn't allow his feelings about that event to pass too quickly; by setting aside time for grieving and honoring that time, it didn't encompass every moment of his life. In the Native American tradition, death is honored as a part of the cycle of life.

Loss is stressful and devastating for all of us, but if we're aware, there can be beauty in honoring those who have passed on as well. In our busy culture, we've removed the rituals of death from our grieving process. We take a few days off when someone we love dies, and then it's back to business, quite often as a coping mechanism. We're taught to suppress our grieving beyond a quick answer of "Fine" when someone asks, "How are you feeling?"

Yes, it might make you feel better to distract yourself from the loss, perhaps not even really experiencing it, by jumping right back into your routine. It's hard to focus on the fact that your mother is really gone when you throw yourself back into a schedule of reports, meetings, and business trips. I'm the first one to know that work needs to be done, but I do believe that this behavior just puts a Band-Aid on a major wound in life.

Only you know how much time is right to spend grieving. It doesn't have to be six or seven years as in some cultures, but I do believe it should be a set time where you "clear the decks" as much as possible to focus on your own feelings instead of declaring that you're "too busy" to deal with it. An aware life includes dealing with both the ups and downs of human existence, including death.

Having No Fear of Death

I'm at the age where friends are dealing with elderly parents and their health issues. Sadly, a friend of mine recently lost her mother, but she was lucky that she could spend the last two weeks of her mother's life with her in the hospital with few interruptions. It was a tough time together but a bonding one, as my friend actually watched her mother take her last breath, fearlessly walking into death. A few nights later, my friend began to see her mother in her dreams, which was unusual, as she'd never dreamed of her mother in the past. I've found that the dream state is a great place to open your mind to anything, including the fact that no one ever truly leaves us if we want to keep them in our lives.

I know from my near-death experience that death isn't frightening, but simply a shift of existences where you don't have a body anymore. As I wrote in a previous chapter, my experience is that this is a realm of pure consciousness. What's on the Other Side is the most peaceful place I've ever known. It's boundless, and you can be any place you choose because you see everything and everywhere in that state. Even with my NDE, I knew that the only hard part of death was for those we would leave behind.

It's quite freeing to live in a way that doesn't fear death. Of course I can only tell you of my own experience, and each individual won't know until they "know." I also know that being at peace about your life being finite is a way to do all you need to do while you're here.

AWARISM

Death is the hardest for the living, and I wish it wasn't such a one-way door. Yet I know from my NDE that the transition of fading into this state of expanded consciousness is very peaceful.

My husband recently lost his beloved grandmother, and I was by his side during the last weeks of her life.

What I found amazing is that his grandmother looked so peaceful even though she was quite ill. There came a moment when I looked into her beautiful face, and I saw that all the lines and wrinkles accumulated over her 96 years had actually softened. It made me think that perhaps our stress holds those lines and wrinkles in place, but when we truly let go, even our outer layer relaxes as we head toward pure consciousness.

Jon was very sad about the passing of his Grandma Fritzi, but he knew from my NDE that leaving a sick body that was so confining was the best thing for her, as she'd be slipping into another existence that was free and expansive. With that understanding in mind, we tried our best not to talk of her impending death as a sad event, but as a way of transcendence or slipping into a completely different dimension. We spent the last few days of her life at her home celebrating her and laughing at funny memories as we watched her dance back and forth on either side of the thin veil that separates life and the Other Side.

I was transfixed as I would watch her talk to loved ones and say "Harry" is here or mention the beautiful sounds of bells ringing. It truly was an unforgettable experience. Yes, it is sad to see someone go whom you love so much, and it doesn't seem right when a disease takes such a good person and even seems unjust. But the memory of seeing Grandma Fritzi drift in and out of such a peaceful place was comforting nonetheless.

It's no wonder to me that the living find it hardest to let go while those who are dying are often quite peaceful about going. Even in a case like mine during an accident, I elevated out of the pain into an altered state of consciousness, where I was quite accepting about going to a different level. At the same time, I disconnected from my pain sensors in the body and brain—this meant that I was literally in no pain at all, because pain simply didn't exist. As I traveled toward a place of complete love, my only concern was for the living including Jon, but rest assured that I was completely fine.

Similarly, my friend who was crushed by the wave in Bali had the experience of peacefully drifting into another expanded dimension as his body lay on the beach with a broken neck. He said he had to make a conscious choice to stay because the alternative was very appealing. We felt him grappling with this decision as we held him on the beach, and his body seemed to deflate as he drifted off. He later told us he had chosen to stay because of his love for his wife.

Knowing all of this can make the living feel a little more at peace about losing loved ones. No, they won't be here to touch, but they are entering a place where consciousness is boundless. If you're losing a loved one, try to see that person in this beautiful place while knowing that in your own life, you will still see them everywhere—in the clouds, in the mountains, in a book you read, in a warm cup of coffee on a cold day. You will feel them everywhere.

Dealing with Loss as a Family

I've always loved the Robin Williams movie *What Dreams May Come*, about a family coping with the afterlife. After seeing that movie, I made a little deal with Jon and Kayla about how we could communicate with each other after we were gone. For instance, I told Kayla that each time she saw a unique cloud shape, like a heart or an animal, I would be communicating with her in some way. Even now, we like to play games and make characters out of the cloud formations. My daughter told me she would communicate through flowers. Jon and I agreed that the unique rush we felt during mountain biking would be our way to communicate with each other. I do have to say that an awareness that life is finite wasn't a depressing topic to tackle for the three of us, but rather the opportunity for a deep discussion that affirmed our love was endless. It might be a beautiful exercise to do with your own family.

Many callers tell me that they get signs from lost loved ones all the time, including that one tulip that blooms although none were planted or smelling a certain scent of someone who passed years ago. These are comforting reminders that the human spirit never truly dies!

One note about flowers and those who have passed: Many spiritual leaders on my show have reminded me that flowers are special in that they have a very high frequency of energy. Roses are one of the most high-frequency flowers, but common houseplants also have a very high vibration as well. Many believe that those who have passed do communicate through flowers and plants that grow, thrive, or even show up at unexpected times or in unexpected places.

This makes me think about a friend who lost her father. He loved to plant red geraniums, and suddenly she started seeing those exact flowers everywhere she went the following spring and summer. She believed that those flowers were an attempt by him to reach out to his loved ones.

AWARISM

A great place to connect with lost ones is through your dreams. Remember that when you're in a dream state, you're detached from your conscious mind, and I believe you are freer to float to different dimensions.

There are many traditions and rituals surrounding death. If you want to visit a gravestone, I believe it's a lovely ritual to honor someone who has passed on. In my heart, I don't believe the person is there trapped in a coffin. Yet if you're grieving and need this as a place to go to be closer to the person you've lost, then by all means visit your relative at the gravesite. Any ritual where you honor the love you shared is beautiful, meaningful, and healing, as most of us like to do something involving action—a visit, flowers, and so forth—to show our love.

It's lovely that on Memorial Day, we honor fallen soldiers, and on Mother's Day there are seas of flowers placed by loving relatives at the graves of their lost loved ones. There are some people who lovingly care for their relatives' graves all year long, making sure that the snow is removed or flowers are present. If the act of doing something makes you more aware of your bond, then absolutely do it.

I'd like to offer another suggestion based on a wonderful family that I've come to know who lost their beloved grandmother, Mae. When Grandma Mae was alive, she would visit this family every Tuesday night for dinner, which inevitably led to her teaching her grandchildren how to bake. What came out of these sessions included the wonderful, intoxicating smells of fresh chocolate-chip cookies and apple pies.

The first Tuesday after Mae passed was a very sad, reflective time for everyone in the family, as they missed Mae so much and the life lessons she shared during baking. It even seemed strange for the house to be devoid of those wonderful smells. A few weeks passed, and then one of the children had the great idea to continue the tradition. "On Tuesday nights," she said, "let's have a family time to honor Grandma. We might not be able to make a cake like she did, but we can still bake together."

Now when the parents come home from work on Tuesdays, there is a family dinner (sticking with tradition), and then they all bake something together. When the eggs hit the floor or the pie is sort of lopsided, the family laughs about it. And while they're baking, they retell stories Mae told them while sharing their lives. That's Grandma Mae's lasting legacy to this family.

Sure, it's hard when you can't pick up a phone and talk to your deceased loved ones because they're not physically there, but having the memory in your heart is also very good as you remain aware of their lasting impact on your life.

FINAL AWARISMS:

* There are five stages of grief that American psychiatrist and pioneer in death studies Elisabeth Kübler-Ross discusses: *denial, anger, bargaining, depression,* and *acceptance.* Please don't try to rush through any of these stages, as each one is to be experienced. Be aware of your emotions and allow yourself the time to move naturally through each step. Especially note that the stages do not go sequentially, but rather skip around in no apparent order and often repeat themselves. When you're not rushing the process, you'll know when it's time to move on.

* One of the best things you can do to deal with grief is set up some sort of ritual where you can still communicate with your lost loved one. It might be by focusing on a

candle or taking a walk. During these times, tell your loved one what you miss about them the most.

* Make sure to spend time with those you love who are still here. Time is the most precious thing of all.

✳ ✳ ✳

CHAPTER 11

Your Aware Body

When my daughter was five years old, I was really struggling with energy. I was tired all the time, and typically around 3 P.M., I would hit a low like no other time during the day. I started to recognize the pattern and attempted to cope with it, until one day when I felt faint. I had my husband take me to see my doctor, who decided to draw blood to find out what was going wrong. Somehow, I must have been holding on by a thread because I got extremely light-headed from the blood test. I went to the hospital, and after a series of tests, I was diagnosed with *Hashimoto's thyroiditis,* an autoimmune disease. This is a condition that has been in my family for three generations, taking a toll on both my mother and grandmother.

Luckily, I have interviewed Dr. Bruce Lipton, cellular biologist and teacher of epigenetics, for about a decade. I've learned from him that you can turn on the genetic markers of disease from your family history if the environment surrounding the cells is perceived to be a stressful one. The field of epigenetics teaches that your thoughts and perceptions have a direct and significant effect on the cells.

At the time when I felt faint, I was a wife, mother, and self-made entrepreneur, and I had turned on the gene. I was trying to be Supermom, and it was time to take off the cape.

I think many women (and men) today are in this position of believing that we can do it all, and we don't even think of asking for help. Over time, this cape-wearing mentality can lead to adrenal-gland burnout. Everything comes crashing down—including our hormones—because of the chronic stress of burning the candle at both ends and trying to be everything to everybody.

In my experience, my get-up-and-go got up and went. It was a huge effort to do the things I was used to doing, such as work out, or even get the energy up to return phone calls or make decisions. While the songs on the radio were talking about swinging from the chandeliers, my energy was plummeting, which made my chances of having a second child very slim.

Hashimoto's is a difficult disease to pinpoint, as the symptoms include common complaints such as fatigue, depression, digestive issues, weight gain, thinning hair and hair loss, and hormonal fluctuations. You can take any one of these symptoms and fool yourself with over-the-counter solutions. Instead, it's better to visit your doctor and get a proper diagnosis by getting tested.

When my daughter was younger, I visited an endocrinologist who'd give me a prescription of Synthroid and tell me to come back in six months, at which point all he would do is increase the dosage. No one was addressing the root cause of my thyroid dysfunction, which was directly linked to my hormonal imbalance.

Since I am a person who likes to get to the bottom of things, and I am ferociously curious when it comes to my own health, I made the decision to do something about the Hashimoto's. As you may have noticed, I am a very divinely guided person because I constantly stay connected with Spirit. I'm always talking to the God of my heart about the direction I'm moving in. I ask to be guided in the right direction, and I make sure to co-create with the universe by doing plenty of research and staying in a place of action, rather than complaint. So now I asked the universe to present me with a viable solution.

After a lot of research and a commitment to not live with the stress of this disease, a doctor e-mailed to tell me that he was specializing in reversing the symptoms of many of his patients with Hashimoto's thyroiditis, including his own wife. I looked on Dr. Gil Kajiki's website and saw the testimonials of the people who had similar symptoms to mine and were experiencing the reversal of many of their symptoms. I replied to him, and later invited him to be a guest on my show. The radio show we did was so popular that Dr. Kajiki said people contacted him from all over the world to talk about his protocol for Hashimoto's. It seemed to make a lot of sense.

I decided to try out Dr. Kajiki's protocol myself, which was a strict four-month plan in accordance with many of the health professionals I had interviewed in the past. It's mostly about using food as medicine. Here, I'd be eliminating what was causing inflammation in my body and igniting the immune-system response to attack my thyroid, which is the definition of Hashimoto's.

I had already eliminated wheat from my diet several years prior, but I had done it to lose weight, which never happened. One of the symptoms of Hashimoto's is stubborn weight loss. By stubborn, I mean I tried everything I knew to lose those last eight pounds of baby weight, and they would just not come off.

Dr. Kajiki's protocol is about getting the proper testing done, which allowed me to gain awareness about my own body. Through blood, urine, stool, and saliva testing, I was able to identify my personal triggers that caused the Hashimoto's to inflame in my body; then I worked on eliminating those triggers.

The foods that I identified to cause inflammation in my body included: wheat and all grains, soy, dairy, corn, and nightshade vegetables (such as potatoes, onions, red and green peppers, and eggplant). These foods are coincidentally the most commonly genetically modified crops in America.

I also learned the link between thyroid and hormones and managed to balance them by following the plan of eating every four hours, and only eating protein and vegetables for the first four months. There is so much more involved here, but I was able to significantly reduce the symptoms of Hashimoto's and regain my energy to normal levels as well as lose my unwanted weight.

In the beginning, I was looking at my new lifestyle as lacking what I wanted rather than supporting my health. But then one of the most motivating factors I learned from Dr. Kajiki was that someone with thyroid disease and Hashimoto's, or any other autoimmune dysfunction, has a 70 percent chance of getting a secondary autoimmune dysfunction. This meant my chances were 70 percent higher of having a very poor quality of life in my later years if I didn't do something—and I wanted to have the energy to watch my daughter grow and to actively participate in her life.

I believe that the mind and the body need to work together, so I used hypnosis to achieve success. I worked with my friend Chris Howard, who is a master of Transformational Hypnosis, to embed in my mind the positive patterns I wanted to have that would improve the quality of my health, including eating the right foods for my body and enjoying them. To this day, I enjoy my current food protocol and my newfound energy.

What Works for Your Body

When it comes to the best eating plan, I can't tell you what's right for your body. The truth is you have to figure that one out on your own because everyone is different. For instance, I don't eat red meat because . . . well, I've never really eaten it. I just don't like the taste of it. It's the same way for me with sour foods, which I detest. And I've determined that certain foods, like green and yellow peppers, tomatoes, potatoes, and all other nightshades, don't work for my body. When I eat them, I feel sluggish and my stomach responds in a negative and often violent way. I love sweet potatoes and eat them several times a week, but don't like the taste or feeling after eating white potatoes.

I ultimately discovered that my digestive system is better off with whole, clean foods that are not genetically modified or filled with toxins.

It's quite helpful to keep a journal to write down how your body responds after eating certain foods. I also recommend doing a food-sensitivity test to help you and your family determine the specifics. This is particularly helpful with children, so they don't spend decades eating things that cause their immune system to work overtime.

Ask yourself: Do you have high energy after eating? Do you feel sluggish? Does your stomach easily digest certain foods? Or do you suddenly feel like enough gas has inflated your gut that you seem pregnant? It's about being conscious of what goes into your mouth because you don't want your body filled with toxins.

Rid your life of foods that don't work for you, and then plan your meals accordingly. If you are busy and will be out most of the day, try to pack your food ahead of time. I always have a protein shake and shaker in my car in case I'm stuck without food and about to hit a blood-sugar low. Sometimes my days are very full, as I go from executive to mom to wife, back to executive, then back to wife and mom again. I'm sure many of you know this drill. Even so, I remember that low blood sugar is very damaging to the thyroid and can be avoided by having protein every four hours. I keep my blood sugar balanced throughout the day because if it tanks, so does everything else.

> ### AWARISM
> It's up to you to figure out what foods work for you and your family, but vow that you will not eat anything that takes you back to a toxic and unconscious place.

If you've decided to try a gluten-free lifestyle, one of the most common things to do is to immediately go out and buy all of the gluten-free foods you see so that you're not missing out on anything. Yet most of these items that are currently on the market contain too many different grains all in one product, which can be equally as distressing on the digestive system.

Some can contain potato starch, brown rice flour, tapioca powder, quinoa dust, and some type of guar gum to bind it all together. Would you ever sit down to eat a plate of all-white foods like potatoes, rice, corn, and tapioca?

Not likely. So why would you eat all of that in one slice of bread? When you chose your gluten-free products, make sure to choose the ones with minimal ingredients.

Become Aware of Your Eating Lifestyle

Many of us have gone fat-free or sugar-free or gluten-free as we try to process the latest health news and adapt to what everyone else tells us is the right way to eat. The only way to really know where you are in your eating habits is to check in with *yourself*—again, it's all about awareness.

One of the best techniques I have used is this: Buy a little notebook that you keep on you 24 hours a day. It goes everywhere with you, including the car, work, and room to room in the house. Each time you eat or drink anything, you must write it down and the time you eat it. This includes your little snacks or sneak foods. If you eat two spoonfuls of mac and cheese from your child's plate, you need to write it down. If you take a big sip of her chocolate smoothie, then it goes in your book. This is especially helpful if you're working out like crazy but never seem to lose weight. My workout burns over 600 calories, for instance, but I wasn't losing any weight—this simply meant that I was eating too much *and* eating the wrong foods for my body.

Note that if you're grabbing food on the go, you're probably unconsciously eating much more than you think. You can't fix the problem until you truly identify what you're doing, so pay close attention over the span of a week or two. At the end of this time period, you will easily be able to pinpoint the unnecessary and often unhealthy calories that you're consuming, perhaps without even knowing it. Do you come home and have a glass of wine? Do you eat a handful of crackers while you answer e-mail? While you're making your child's lunch, do you eat the peanut butter off the knife? Once you know the issue, you can easily do a pattern interrupt.

AWARISM

Stop tricking yourself and insisting that you're older now and your metabolism is certainly slowing down. Although this could be medically true, you're also probably eating too much. There are plenty of amazingly fit and healthy 40-, 50-, 60-, and 70-year-olds who can serve as our role models.

Aware Exercise

I exercise in order to feel good, regulate my system, and heal faster. As you know, I need to get my blood flowing. Now, that doesn't necessarily mean mountain-bike racing—but a nice, easy, slow, long-distance ride does wonderful things for me these days. I also love my spinning class and instructor, so we train together a couple days a week to lift my mood and sweat out toxins.

Basically, I'm someone who wakes up not even knowing her first name, so I need to drink a little water and get on the bike to kick my system into gear. Literally.

If I'm traveling, I'll still get 30 minutes of moving in—the point is to work up a sweat because the brain chemicals released during even a short workout gets me functioning. If I don't work out early in the morning, I know I won't operate at full throttle that day, and that's reason enough to get me going.

I make working out an essential part of my morning routine. I drive my daughter to school and the minute I leave that car-pool area, I'm off to the gym or home for a bike ride. Yes, I really do want to just go grab a cup of coffee or even try to fall back asleep, but I don't. At the gym, I'll start by walking on the treadmill for 10 minutes to wake my brain up again, and 15 minutes later, I'm running or jogging while thinking about what I need to do that day.

I have great ideas while I'm working out, which is another plus for getting in that early- morning movement. I also work out with four other women and an incredibly positive trainer, and we keep each other totally accountable as we're coached through our routines. It's usually two of us on the treadmill with the other two doing weights and then we switch.

By the end of 60 minutes, I'm drenched in sweat and completely spent, but still mentally ready to charge into my day. I'll go on to work on my show or on a coaching call or whatever else the day calls for, knowing that I've done something wonderful for myself to get the entire process in motion.

> **AWARISM**
>
> There is something empowering about getting your workout done early in the day, because you did it—check that off the daily list—and then you don't have to worry as the day backs up that you'll never get to it. If you get it done in the early morning, then you're golden, while also setting up your brain for a great day thanks to the endorphins and oxygen.

I believe that exercise is incredibly healing, both mentally and physically. You can feel the chemistry in your body changing as your blood flows and you release dopamine and serotonin.

There is a reason why cyclists are so addicted to the bike, because we know that our bodies and minds are healing and working at maximum levels while we fly across the dirt. But you don't have to be a work-out-aholic to get this release, as 10 to 20 minutes of movement will get you there.

> **AWARISM**
>
> The chemicals released during a workout stimulate the production of neurotransmitters that are used for maximum brain function. In other words, exercise helps you to think more clearly.

My Daily Eating Plan

This is my basic daily eating plan for maximum awareness:

* **Breakfast:** I have a green drink during my workout, made from a powered mix that is the equivalent of nine salads diluted with a lot of water. Then I drink 20 oz. of pure water as I'm working out. Afterward, I have a protein shake to assimilate nutrients.

* **Lunch:** I have a protein shake if I'm on the run, or a healthy salad with a chicken breast if I'm eating lunch out.

* **Dinner:** I have some healthy grilled protein, vegetables, and a salad.

* **Snacks:** I like fresh lean turkey wrapped around cucumber slices, or low-sugar fruit like apple or plum slices. I love Donna Gates's cultured vegetables as a probiotic and digestive aid; they're also great for reducing inflammation and getting rid of yeast.

FINAL AWARISMS:

* Eat every three to four hours, and always include some kind of protein. This is essential for keeping your metabolism fired up and for feeding muscle, which in turn burns fat.

* Try avoiding wheat for a week and see what that does for your body and energy levels.

* It has been said a million times, but for a reason: Drink at least 80 ounces of water a day, or half your body weight in ounces.

* When you're hungry, you're usually thirsty. Our bodies are 80 percent water, as is our brain. Drink, drink, drink.

* Every single day, you must move your blood with exercise. You are releasing neurotransmitters that make your brain happy, including serotonin. Exercise also brings joy and happiness into your life.

* Keep in mind that dairy causes mucus to develop within your system. I do love cheese, but eat it only occasionally because it's not good for my body.

* Don't use time as an excuse for eating poorly. If you want a healthy snack, then take a piece of turkey and wrap it around sliced cucumber; or make a wrap from turkey, spinach leaves, and some avocado or a few dried cranberries. Cook extra salmon and cut into squares to have the next day with lettuce and spinach for lunch. Delicious!

* Limit your sugar intake and get your sweetness from whole sources like fruit or a bit of honey.

* Avoid nuts that are dry roasted, as most of them are rancid by the time they reach your supermarket shelf.

* ✳ *

CHAPTER 12

Aware and in Love

Love relationships are such a big part of our shared experiences as humans that I wanted to address them in this book, but from a different angle of awareness.

Most of us will come to learn that nothing in life makes us quite as aware of ourselves as being in a relationship with someone else. It's almost as if the floodgates open, and our own issues come to the surface. All of a sudden, we're seeing patterns in ourselves that we were never conscious of before, although they were most likely there all the time. Human beings don't tend to notice or embrace our true patterns, but love has a sneaky way of taking a giant yellow highlighter to them.

As you've read, I've come a long way from being a workaholic who was emotionally absent to falling in love and honoring my relationship with my husband, while striving to be as emotionally present as possible for us as a couple. Am I perfect? Far from it. For example, I never realized what a neat freak I was until Jon and I got married, although I always did embrace organization and cleanliness. Now the neat freak in me seems to have hit overdrive—there are mornings when I actually find myself running late to an appointment because I'm stuck in the kitchen straightening up one last thing or making sure that dish reaches the cabinets instead of sitting in the drainer all day long.

Jon knows (only too well) that I love order in our house, but he is the exact opposite. For instance, he'll take off certain articles of clothing and throw them in the kitchen. I can barely even type those words without running in there right now to see if we have a pileup by the stove. "Honey, the kitchen is not a closet," I will gently remind him, nudging his gaze to the floor, where a pair of socks are resting from their long day out in the world. "There are socks on the floor," I'll say in the most even voice possible.

Of course, Jon will eventually pick them up. What annoys him—and what I needed him to point out to me— is when my obsession with order causes me to talk about socks first thing after we haven't seen each other all day. "What about a hug?" he'll say.

I have become aware of where I was going wrong here as a partner. Sure, I need those socks to relocate, but there is a much better way to approach this situation: Hugs, love, kisses, and incentives. What about a rewards program? It sounds funny, but the truth is my husband feels hurt when I focus on his socks before I focus on him. This has been an important lesson that, once realized, really helped us not let a misunderstanding fester.

AWARISM

Are you endlessly badgering your mate about money, schedules, or family issues? Check the nag meter. Make sure you soften your wants and desires with meaningful hugs and sincere conversation before you launch into your most pressing annoyance. It will be better for both of you in the long run, and you each might get what you want.

A True Partnership

Jon and I have built a marriage where we are equal in most ways, but we know that the other person's strong shoulder is always there. The key is we take turns leaning on each other as we walk side by side through life. It's not about carrying the other, which can be construed as a codependent relationship. I believe that relying on a true partner in life means that you share things and support each other.

Yet as much as we are equals, I can't honestly say that we share the entire responsibilities of our lives or our household in a 50-50 way. I've found that when you have children, more of the daily duties seem to fall on the female, including driving, homework, and meal prep. It's in women's DNA to nurture, although men like my husband also have a strong need for this, which is why he is such a great dad—he does things a different way. So, as we walk together, I know that it won't always be 50-50 in terms of parenting or housecleaning. I have different needs than Jon in those regards; but we don't judge each other about it.

> ### AWARISM
> Even when you share things in an equal relationship, it's never going to be 100 percent equal. Knowing and accepting this fact avoids resentment.

I'm very strong in our relationship, and so is my husband, with the key being that we allow each other to be that strong. We're also available to make sure that the other doesn't sail off the cliff. For example, I often have a million ideas and jump right into action because I want to get it done. However, if I get too carried away or start going down what Jon considers to be the wrong path, he'll check in with me and let me know that things are getting a bit out of control. At the same time, he accepts that I love to take charge because that's who I am. He lets me be me . . . but when it's too much, he'll say in the most loving way possible, and with a smile on his face, "Yep, there's Lisa again and her fierce will. Down, tiger, down!'"

In that moment, I know that I have to consider the situation and most likely turn it down a few notches as I allow my deep-thinking partner to join in, and help me make better-informed choices from a different perspective.

We do this without judgment, as pointing fingers is the first step toward resentment. Jon would never say, "Oh, there's my wife rushing right into the fire." And I would never say, "There's my methodical husband making this decision take forever." We're a good team because we realize that we have different personality traits, and know that this is what makes us unstoppable.

I embrace the fact that my husband reads everything three times, making sure that we're on solid ground, even if that planning and research takes time. He has a much more detail-oriented mind than I do, and I appreciate that his strength is my weakness and vice versa. He loves the fact that I have the big-picture mind that moves us in the right direction, but I don't always pay attention to the details. Instead of allowing ourselves to look at the negatives (I want to rush; he wants to mull over), we know what we're in for because this is the person we married. We celebrate our true selves in this relationship knowing that as a whole we're better than individual parts.

Are you aware of your own mate's amazing traits? Instead of thinking of him as a neat freak, why not rejoice because he keeps order in the house so that you can be creative in other areas? Instead of lamenting that she can't say no to others, why not be grateful that you married someone with such a big heart? When you're truly aware in your relationship, you look for the positives and don't turn them into negatives (most of the time). And as you become aware of your differences as a couple, you can work out what bugs you.

I love to stay long at parties and family gatherings, for instance, while Jon is the type who loves to leave early. After several disagreements on this topic, we agreed to take separate cars to many of these events—so when he gets tired and wants to go home, he can leave and I can stay. It's a win-win for both of us.

AWARISM
Don't make it so that only one person has to win at a situation. Look for the win-wins where *everyone* is happy and feels as if their needs are being met as long as there is communication about the issue.

I'm constantly hearing that in these busy times, couples just don't have the quality time to spend with each other or their children. Once you're aware of the time crunch, it's helpful to make formal plans to do fun things or important ones. I believe that every busy family needs a calendar. When you make it official, it's important, and the other person knows that they need to show up so there are no surprises. It helps if you both work to respect each other's time.

Jon and I have set up a shared calendar on our phones and send each other invites to do things if it's in the middle of a busy week. If at the last minute our daughter needs a ride from school and I can't make it, I'll send him a calendar invite for that. If she has a soccer game or horse show, it goes on the calendar.

My husband and I are the dynamic duo when we align our energies. Two is more powerful than one in my mind when it comes to creating something. For example, if we brainstorm together on how to fix a problem, it will get fixed. If we work together to create a change in one of our businesses, it always turns out better than expected. One example was to help a friend who was very sick. We both combined our contacts and knowledge and had our friend connected with several specialists and a green-juice delivery service in a very short amount of time.

Combine and create is a much better motto than divide and conquer in our lives.

Pulling Together in Challenging Times

How do you stay aware in your relationship when a serious concern crops up? For example, I wanted to move to a new house but Jon wanted to stay put in our old home. He finally agreed to move, which was just the beginning of a very challenging time for us.

As I mentioned previously, we had a hard time selling our original house, which meant that finances were suddenly tight. But my husband never said, "Why the hell are we doing this? What were you thinking?" I have to admit that those were lines I said to myself during this very stressful period of our lives.

Jon didn't make me feel bad for a decision I pushed our family into when it came to relocating. In fact, he made a very intentional, aware decision not to blame me during the tense moments. Why? We were already in it. We are in everything together. So what if one of us makes a tough choice that might even be wrong? We find our way as a couple and remain supportive of each other. Our attitude remained, "Okay, there is no point in pointing fingers. We have some issues in our lives now like getting rid of this first house. Let's do it together."

> ## AWARISM
> When you focus on action instead of blame as a couple, you will grow from challenges rather than allowing them to weaken you.

In the end, it's six months post-move as I write this, and we are so grateful that we changed our lives with this new house. Everything is incredible in our new dwelling, and all of the tough moments were certainly worth it. During the move, when one of us got overwhelmed, the other would be there to pick them up and vice versa. We were never both down at the same time; instead, when one was weak, the other was strong.

Again, we never made each other feel bad, but simply said, "This needs attention. I'll go ahead and pick up the phone." That's much different than saying (even to yourself), "Why didn't my husband do this?"

If you pick up the slack for your partner, then it all works out, as long as you both learn from your mistakes and don't repeat bad habits that get you in difficult positions. Accountability is key in a good relationship.

Relationship Killers

Naturally, we all slip thanks to a hectic week or work troubles or other life stresses. However, there are certain things that many of us do that I classify under "relationship killers." These are little problems that go on to become routine, thus seriously undermining your quest to have a good and loving relationships.

Let's explore a few ways you can become more aware in these areas:

1. Are you aware that you constantly complain?

Most of us know the scenario. It's been a super stressful day filled with job challenges, plus the car didn't start and you have to drive to soccer practice. You pick up your child and find out that she has a mountain of homework tonight, and the mail contains a letter from the IRS informing you that you have a penalty. It's been a pressure-cooker day, to say the least.

When your mate walks through the door and asks, "How was your day?" you don't hesitate. You just let it rip: "I really can't take it anymore from my boss, and that mechanic tried to rip us off again. I don't like Ashley's teacher this year because she's so tough. You're going to have to do the math homework because I have to write a report tonight for my meeting. And can you please walk the dog . . . who, incidentally, ate a bunch of the socks today."

Time out. Take a breath. Try to think about how you just sounded, because no one wants to walk through the door only to be faced by the Super Complainer. Yes, there are several important daily issues that you will discuss with your mate, but you have to think twice before unveiling the laundry list of complaints all the time. Certainly you're upset about all of the above, but when you're the constant and chronic complainer in the family, it gets old really fast and kills romance and love.

I'm just like you in that I can get caught in the complaining rut, and Jon is great at calling me out on it. He'll let me vent and then say, in a very calm voice, "Do you realize you're complaining a lot?" The truth is I hadn't realized it because it can be strangely addictive—you can go from a part-time complainer to a chronic one pretty quickly. I'm actually quite glad when Jon calls me out on this because I don't want to be that person in our relationship. When I need to vent, that's what good girlfriends and my mom are for.

To become more aware, you might need to make a deal with your partner that they do call you out. And then try to deal with some of the load by yourself and complain when necessary or turn your complaint into a joke. "I guess our mechanic is allowing us to help him buy that new house with what he charged for that muffler," I'll tell Jon, and we'll laugh. Most of our complaints aren't so big that we can't chuckle about them.

2. If you're a woman, are you aware that you're treating your husband like a girlfriend?

When it comes to relationships, there is absolutely a difference between a man in your life and another friend. Yes, your husband or significant other should be looked at as your best friend, but he's still not your *girlfriend,* meaning that he doesn't want you to just drone on and on about that one thing. It's not that you shouldn't talk to your partner about your feelings, hopes, fears, and concerns. That's part of a relationship. But all women know that we speak with our girlfriends differently and dig for the very marrow of every situation. Becoming aware as a woman is to realize that this drives your guy absolutely nuts.

(For men reading this book, it's also helpful to know that your woman is used to sharing a lot of information, so pull up a chair and please listen.)

One of my favorite relationship experts, Alison Armstrong, says not to treat your man like a very hairy girlfriend. In other words, don't go on and on with what happened at your child's school that day or at the gym. Most psychologists will agree that men operate in a mode where they want to hear what's going on . . . and then they want to fix it. As you're speaking, your man is thinking, *How can I fix this? Do I need to fix this? What is my action item?* When you drone on, you're interrupting his fix-it plan. In fact, you're frustrating him because he wants action and you want to drown in more words that are, in fact, impeding the action.

An aware relationship celebrates our differences as men and women and accommodates them. When I tell Jon a longer story, he stops me and asks, "Do you want me to do something about this situation or just listen?" If I tell him to listen, he is happy to do so without the need to fix something. It actually works out quite well.

3. Are you aware that your job in a disagreement is to resolve it and then move on?

It's not realistic to think that you will never fight with your mate, no matter how much in love you are. If you have zero conflicts, then someone is trying to suppress their feelings instead of becoming aware. I believe it's important to calmly talk about what's bothering you with one caveat: get it out quickly, and get over it just as fast!

Confession: I'm like most women in that I like to sulk when I'm mad at my husband. Sometimes I even want to go to bed mad because it's part of the wallowing process! But Jon refuses to let me do it. He reaches deep and pulls me out of my sulking pattern (and it is a pattern many girls develop in childhood).

I have always had a hard time expressing my truth, based on not feeling safe to do so as a child. However, now that I am an accountable adult living in the present time, expressing my truth is my best medicine. Sometimes I need to sit down with my husband and force myself to talk things out in a calm matter so I feel fully expressed and don't hold my feelings inside. I do it in a way that is not accusatory, and Jon appreciates that more than me hiding it inside and blowing up later for something small. How many of you do this?

Another powerful question to ask yourself if something is pushing your buttons is: What issue do you have in yourself that bothers you about your mate? In other words, what are you projecting onto them that deep down bothers you about yourself? For example, if I have a judgment about Jon watching too much TV, what issue inside of *me* is unresolved—could it be that I feel I don't have enough time for myself to chill and resent that he does? After exploring this issue in myself, I dropped the judgment of my husband and honor his downtime watching TV.

This is a great way of being aware of an issue, solving it, and then moving on without allowing it to erode the relationship or yourself inside. Think of it this way: You're in a relationship, and you want to both work together toward a solution instead of secretly enjoying the drama of it all.

4. Are you aware that you're "in business" together, so you need to make the business of your relationship work for you?

Jon and I like to have life-planning meetings when it comes to our family. We don't sit down in the boardroom or even at our kitchen table, but prefer to jump on our mountain bikes, where we have some of our greatest brain-storming sessions. If I'm bothered about something, we'll get on our bikes, and I'll talk it over with him. We even do this just to ask each other how things are going.

It's absolutely worth it to get a kid sitter, get out of the house, and get on a bike (walking also works) to really talk. The outdoors is a great space to do this, as it is so con-ducive to dreaming big for our "company"—our family. Mountain biking is also our place of spiritual connection. We bond with each other and nature while we're on our bikes. We sometimes bring our daughter on a ride with us and let our collective spirits fly together.

We can also get a bit crazy on these "field trips." The other day, I was angry about my reluctance to say no, which had caused me to overschedule myself. All of a sud-den, we were on our bikes and I said, "I need to learn the art of saying no!" Jon encouraged me to start practicing—right now.

"No, no, no!" I screamed into the world.

"I love to hear you say that!" he joked.

Now, we both laugh about it because we're lucky no one was passing us and thought that I was in trouble, screaming "No!"

5. Are you aware that your partner who doesn't want to talk really does?

A lot of women call in to the show to tell me that they want to talk about issues with their man, but he's "just not good at talking." If you're aware of this in your own rela-tionship, the key is to draw him out because deep down, there is probably a talker lurking underneath that macho exterior.

Never say the killer words: *We have to talk.* That just shuts a non-talkative mate down to zero. If you do need to talk to this type of partner, give him a little time and space. Then take this person into his own arena, meaning do something he likes to do like go on a car ride or take a walk by the lake. When you bring a non-talkative partner (man or woman) into an environment that makes him or her feel comfortable, the words will flow much easier.

FINAL AWARISMS:

* Don't over-talk a situation with your mate who just wants to jump into action.

* Look for opportunities to leave the house, get out in nature, and talk over what's going on in your lives.

* Agree to have time where you disconnect from technology to really focus on each other.

* Don't treat your husband like your girl-friend, or whine and complain needlessly —and certainly not when he's just walked in the door.

* * *

CHAPTER 13

The Aware Child

I don't claim to be an expert in child rearing, but I have learned so much from *The Aware Show* and by raising my own consciousness levels in this area. I do know with absolute certainty that the crucial factor in raising a self-confident, aware child is that they must know beyond any doubt that they are loved. That's my number one bit of parenting advice: *Let your child know every single day that the love starts here.*

AWARISM
I believe that you should let your child know that they are loved, but also that they are accepted here in this family. Love plus acceptance is an amazing combination for a child as they develop into an adult.

Another crucial part of parenting for me is listening to my daughter. I treat her like she matters, and her voice has meaning in our household. My husband and I live in a world far from the one that swore by the old adage that children should be seen and not heard. Instead, we welcome our daughter's opinion and truly hear her, which means looking her in the eyes and listening—not texting or staring at a computer screen nodding our heads while she tries to capture our attention.

Children are small by stature, and often their opinion is deemed less worthy by society because they're not mature. I feel that shouldn't be the case; it's so frustrating when you're not heard. That's often why children have tantrums—they can't explain themselves, and their frustration at not being heard builds to the boiling point. You are your child's audience and need to give them the attention they deserve.

I also understand that the years before age seven comprise the imprint period of your child's life. They are literally mirroring everything you do, consciously and unconsciously. They absorb how you talk, your relationships, your eating habits, your relationship with yourself . . . everything.

Sometimes I'm aware of my daughter watching me, and I pay careful attention to my actions. I'm not always paying 100 percent attention, but I try to get it right most of the time. I realized I only had a short amount of time to set up her model of the world and now I am seeing her make good choices (at least most of the time).

AWARISM

When your child expresses an opinion, don't override them or jump in to teach them a lesson. Ask for their opinion often, and allow them to feel heard. Even when they don't completely understand a subject, they still want to express their views. Don't make them feel as if each time they speak, they will be corrected or taught that they are wrong.
In other words, just let them speak while you listen.

Get Physical and Play, Play, Play

In our house, we believe in a lot of hugging and physical contact. You want to tell someone you love them? You say it, and then you hug it out! Another great way to bond with your child is to return to that state of play that *you* once enjoyed. Go ahead and yell, "You're it!" Chase them and goof around together, which is the way that children like to express themselves in their optimal creative zone. Your backyard or local park is made for a game of tag or a race. You can even enjoy a good pillow fight before bed.

I know most families are busy, but I believe it's crucial to build in this fun time so that it becomes the most important activity of the day. It doesn't have to take long— an hour of hard play in the park is worth a million trips to the store or a movie where no one is having any contact with each other. Even older kids will enjoy it once you get them out there in nature.

Another great way to get physical with your child is to rub their feet or back before bed, which calms them and makes them feel safe with Mom's touch before falling asleep. I started this with Kayla when she was little, and it continues to this day as often as we can. It's a sweet, connected way to end our day as a team as we talk about her deepest feelings, the ones she can't tell anyone else. It is a very safe space, especially after a hard soccer game!

How to Help Your Child Deal with Life's Disappointments

I sit on the sidelines of my daughter's soccer games, and when her team loses, I see so many sweet yet long faces trudge off the field. Yes, it truly is the agony of defeat combined with expectations that were not met for that game.

Kayla will sulk to the car, where I always ask her the same question: "What did you learn from the game?" More than once she has answered, "I learned that you really need to work as a team and sometimes if I do my personal best, that's still a victory for me. If I didn't do my best, then I need to use it as fuel for the next game to do better." I am so proud when I hear that's she's taking away some valuable lessons from these disappointments.

A while ago, she tore some ligaments in her foot during a game, and found herself on crutches. This was devastating because she had to miss her big tournament, plus we had to go to the doctor a few times. She was really disappointed, which broke my heart, but I knew as a mother that I had to get past my own sorrow for her losses and teach her how to use awareness to get through this tough time.

First of all, Kayla still wanted to play. The doctor told me that most kids with her type of injury would most likely turn this tear into a chronic injury if they went on to play, and then it would develop into arthritis as they aged. Knowing that she would absolutely not be playing too soon, I told her the truth: "Honey, you will be in your cast for four weeks. We're not taking it off earlier so you can play. You have to heal."

Even at her young age, she went into meltdown mode, and it was my job to be strong for her during an emotional time when she was weak and upset. What we learned to do, through one of my radio-show guests, was to be aware of her healing by visualizing going into her cells. Here's how it works: There are electrical currents or energy in each of the cells, and we learned how to connect to the energetic light in the cells to help reconnect the ones that had been disconnected so that they could grow new tissue.

What you do is get very quiet or into a meditative zone. Imagine that your cells have lights within them. With your mind, go right into the cells of the injured area and think about them healing and reconnecting. While you do this, you don't focus on the injury itself, sweeping those thoughts away. In their place, you only think about white healing light and the cells reconnecting in perfect working order so that the light can shine even brighter. This gives you, and your child, something to focus on instead of the injury.

My daughter and I visualized a space where she knew that her ligaments were torn and disconnected, but also that each cell had an electrical charge or light in it. She affirmed that her entire body was made of these wonderful electrical currents because she was energy. Then she took the energy and the light inside the hurt cells and visualized the cells bonding together in the correct way, creating and then replicating healthy cells. Next, she visualized the electricity bonding the cells together as she sent additional energy to that area to speed up the process.

We did this exercise several times a day and even did it on the sidelines of the soccer field, where Kayla had come to cheer her team on to victory as she hobbled around on her crutches.

It has been proven that you can heal your body through visualization, and there is something so life affirming about taking this action to help heal your cells instead of just doing nothing or feeling sorry for yourself. This technique is also used to reduce pain, and is a great way to find acceptance during a long healing process or when dealing with disease, as you are empowering your own healing.

Adults and children both know that sometimes the worst part of any illness is that powerless feeling, and you're taking your power back in this exercise.

As I write this, my child is 11 years old; however, many of these techniques will work with adult children as well.

Final Awarisms:

* Truly listen to your child without interruption more often than not.

* Reinforce that your child is loved and accepted in the home. One goes with the other.

* Get out there and have fun with your child doing what you loved when you were a kid. Run around a park and get physical. You will enjoy it just as much as the little person shrieking with joy.

* So many people say, "They grow up so fast." It's the truth—so enjoy your child's growing-up process and don't let it pass you by. This is the best part of life, so please be aware and don't miss it!

✻ ✳ ✻

Epilogue

Thank you for reading my book. I hope this has been as inspiring for you to read as it has been for me to write. Living with awareness is one of my greatest blessings. To be able to create an aware life is something I strive for every single day for my family and myself, as well as in my work. I remain grateful for each and every day. May you always have the energy to live the way you want to live in your own life, too.

In your attempt to live an aware life, you will get it right about 80 percent of the time. That's right, I'm saying that 20 percent of the time, you might just mess up. You see, even if you have all the practical tools for awareness in this book, you're human and you're going to slip up. But this is a book about practical awareness and how to use these tools in your everyday, active lifestyle.

There will also be times when something like an almost-tragic bike accident happens, and you'll find that it was one of life's true and greatest blessings. Would I be here in the same way today if my head hadn't hit that rocky mountain terrain, leading to my near-death experience and a completely different outlook on my life? I know the answer is no. And I'm so grateful for what has brought me to this point, including that I healed my brain from a traumatic injury.

I have brought awareness into my life. I don't walk around in a crisis-fueled, stressed-out state where I invite sickness in by weakening my immune system. I enjoy my work, and my family relationship is solid and full of healthy communication. My life has purpose and meaning. I embrace today, and I don't fear tomorrow.

Becoming aware isn't an overnight endeavor, but a process. You can begin by asking yourself, "What is working in my life? What *isn't* working? Where do I want to be five years from now, one year from now, one day from now?"

As I finish this book, there are over three and a half million listeners who tune in and listen to *The Aware Show* every month, and the international audience grows bigger by the day. I wanted to write a book because I've been interviewing some amazing people since 1999, and I love giving them a platform on the air to talk about their work. I never intended to be a host, as I truly came at this career with a deep desire to help myself and other people.

These pages reflect how I've made use of the incredible awareness techniques I've learned to change my own life and transform myself. And I wanted to introduce readers to new modalities including EEG, as a way to learn and heal what's broken. Food and exercise are also essential to your aware life, as taking care of your body is one of the keys.

I'm so passionate about helping people and introducing them to master teachers who have the solutions in every interview I do. Of course, there is so much I couldn't fit into one book, which is why I hope to do many more while I continue to expand the platform of my shows. I feel so blessed when hear from individuals who tell me, "I listened to your show and it has truly changed my life."

We live in an information age, and I love sharing information. I was going to write a book just based on my interviews, but on second thought I decided to tell you my story and how these interviews impacted me. On my shows, I purposely do not share much about myself because I like to give the guest the platform so that their message can shine. So *Becoming Aware* is my chance to tell my story. I hope that in reading it, you and I have gotten a little closer, and that you can gather as much information as possible to make your life more aware.

Now let's get back to our aware goal—I think 80 percent is more than pretty good. I strive to get it right most of the time, and I'm trying to close the gap between that 80 and the leftover 20 every single day. I don't think we can be 100 percent aware unless we're a monk on the top of a mountain. On the ground, we need practical solutions to make our life work, which is what I wanted to share with you in these pages.

I strive.

I am only human.

An *aware* human.

I create in multiple realities and sit down and do visualizations with my family and teams. We turn up the intensity and the emotion and put ourselves into our joyous futures. We give back in gratitude and act as if the future has already happened as we make it our reality. There is not a shadow of a doubt that it won't work out the way I created it. This creates the neural bridges that act as a memory in the brain and thus create neurotransmitters that bond together. That's what a memory is. And then you're suddenly living it as you thrust positively into your future.

Experience what it's like to win the game.
Fall in love.
Live in joy.
As I end every show . . .
Until next time, I invite you to stay *aware*.

Lisa

⁕ ✳ ⁕

Acknowledgments

If I could take this moment to thank all the people who have helped me in my life, I would take up this entire book. So for now, I would like to say thank you to my parents for their love. I would like to thank my loving husband, Jon, and amazing daughter, Kayla, whom I am blessed to love and be loved by every day of my life.

I would like to thank my entire *Aware Show* team, including Gina Salvati, the executive producer of all things *Aware,* and more important, my longtime friend. I am in deep gratitude to Bo Rinaldi for his support of my vision—and an enlightened visionary himself, whom I am honored to know once again in this lifetime. Thanks to Joyce Walker, Cliff Schinkel, and the entire team of Conscious Catalysts behind the engine of *The Aware Show,* who tirelessly present the love and the vision of *Aware* to the world.

I would also like to thank all of the listeners and people who have been courageous enough to change their life in a positive way as a result of something they heard on *The Aware Show.* Know that you are loved, and it is my dream that you will share what you've learned with others and contribute to raising the vibration of this planet.

I would like to thank the countless healers, doctors, visionary leaders, and teachers who have inspired me along the way and brought me back to balance when I needed it the most, many of whom I mention in this book. Specifically, I would like to thank Dr. Wayne Dyer, Reid Tracy, and the entire Hay House family for believing in me and supporting the vision I had from Spirit to communicate messages that inspire positive growth and change. I will always be grateful for your conscious support. I would also like to thank Shannon Littrell and Cindy Pearlman for their guidance on this book.

Finally, I would like to thank my angels and guides, whom I am in constant communication with and who have guided me in the right direction every step of the way. I am a truly guided soul and remain in deep gratitude for the constant support of the divine forces in the universe for the highest good of all involved.

* ✳ *

About the Author

Since 1999, **Lisa Garr** has hosted a popular syndicated radio program called *The Aware Show*. Based on her desire to live in a more conscious world, Lisa created *The Aware Show* to feature best-selling authors and experts in the fields of natural health, cutting-edge science, personal growth, and spirituality. With a background in the healing arts, she is considered an expert herself in the field of lifestyle and transformational media programming. In addition, she comes from a long line of entertainers, including her aunt, actress Teri Garr; and her grandmother, Phyllis Garr, an original Radio City Music Hall Rockette.

Lisa also hosts a show on Hay House Radio called *Being Aware* and a series for Gaiam TV called *Gaiam Inspirations*. She is a regular weekend host on *Coast to Coast AM*, syndicated in over 500 stations around the world, and has one of the largest telesummit series on the Internet. Combined, she reaches millions of listeners globally a month.

Lisa lives with her husband and daughter in Los Angeles, and can be contacted via e-mail: news@theawareshow .com. To listen to *The Aware Show* or learn more about her telesummits, please visit: www.theawareshow.com.

* * *

We hope you enjoyed this Hay House book. If you'd like to receive our online catalog featuring additional information on Hay House books and products, or if you'd like to find out more about the Hay Foundation, please contact:

Hay House, Inc., P.O. Box 5100, Carlsbad, CA 92018-5100
(760) 431-7695 or (800) 654-5126
(760) 431-6948 (fax) or (800) 650-5115 (fax)
www.hayhouse.com® • www.hayfoundation.org

✷ ✷ ✷

Published and distributed in Australia by:
Hay House Australia Pty. Ltd., 18/36 Ralph St., Alexandria NSW 2015
Phone: 612-9669-4299 • *Fax:* 612-9669-4144 • www.hayhouse.com.au

Published and distributed in the United Kingdom by:
Hay House UK, Ltd., Astley House, 33 Notting Hill Gate,
London W11 3JQ • *Phone:* 44-20-3675-2450
Fax: 44-20-3675-2451 • www.hayhouse.co.uk

Published and distributed in the Republic of South Africa by:
Hay House SA (Pty), Ltd., P.O. Box 990, Witkoppen 2068
Phone/Fax: 27-11-467-8904 • www.hayhouse.co.za

Published in India by:
Hay House Publishers India, Muskaan Complex, Plot No. 3, B-2,
Vasant Kunj, New Delhi 110 070 • *Phone:* 91-11-4176-1620
Fax: 91-11-4176-1630 • www.hayhouse.co.in

Distributed in Canada by:
Raincoast Books, 2440 Viking Way, Richmond, B.C. V6V 1N2
Phone: 1-800-663-5714 • *Fax:* 1-800-565-3770 • www.raincoast.com

✷ ✷ ✷

Take Your Soul on a Vacation

Visit www.HealYourLife.com® to regroup, recharge, and reconnect with your own magnificence. Featuring blogs, mind-body-spirit news, and life-changing wisdom from Louise Hay and friends.

Visit www.HealYourLife.com today!